# JACK'S YAK

A unique journey through time with the special trees of the Lake District
and Cumbria and the remarkable stories they have to tell

**KEITH RICHARDSON**
Colour photography by
**VAL CORBETT**

# JACK'S YAK

A unique journey through time with the special trees of the Lake District
and Cumbria and the remarkable stories they have to tell

## KEITH RICHARDSON

Colour photography by
### VAL CORBETT

RIVER
GRETA
WRITER

RIVER
GRETA
WRITER

River Greta Writer
Windebrowe Avenue
Keswick
Cumbria
CA12 4JG

www.rivergretawriter.co.uk

JACK'S YAK
A unique journey through time with the special trees of the Lake District
and Cumbria and the remarkable stories they have to tell

First River Greta Writer edition: 2011

A catalogue record for this book is available from the British Library.
ISBN: 978-0-9559640-2-2

Printed and bound in the UK by The Amadeus Press, Cleckheaton, West Yorkshire.
Design and pre-press by Walker Ellis Associates, Threlkeld, Cumbria.

 WALKER ELLIS ASSOCIATES

# CONTENTS
## Jack's Yak

'. . . and slips of yew, slivered in the moon's eclipse'

The Third Witch in *Macbeth*, Act 4, Scene 1. William Shakespeare

Hawthorn blossom and
bluebells at Grasmere.

*Sunlit woodland at Lowther.*

This book is a one off.

Its beginnings were an interest in trees that goes back as far as my first attempts to climb into the branches of a tree when I was a lad. It appears that most people have a special affection for trees and I suspect it is one that is almost subliminal and, like most things, probably has its origins somewhere in childhood.

I found the idea of writing simply about trees alone far too limiting. So I hit upon the concept of writing a book with a theme line of trees and gave myself the freedom to tap into a wide range of related topics that also interested me. The Rebel Tree at Clifton, near Penrith, resulted in a study of the Jacobite Rebellion of 1745 and the battle and bloodshed that ensued, much of it in the old counties of Cumberland and Westmorland; the spectacular windblown hawthorns on Humphrey Head, looking out over Morecambe Bay and the Levens Estuary, lead to an exploration of the Cumbrian coastline and its shipbuilding and maritime tradition; while the oak on the cricket ground at Lowther Cricket Club gave me the perfect excuse to write about cricket in the Eden Valley and beyond.

Those are just three examples of the way in which the many trees in *Jack's Yak* were the coat hooks on which I took the liberty of hanging a rich variety of material, information and observations, as I embarked on what was to become an amazing journey through time with the trees as signposts en route.

With one exception, the sycamore at Sycamore Gap on Hadrian's Wall, Northumberland, all of the trees are in the Lake District and Cumbria. Not all of the notable trees in this wonderful part of the world are here but I think you will find most of the more exceptional ones in these pages. I hope that the stories will enable you to see this area in a novel and unusual light . . . through words and thoughts, the lens of photographer Val Corbett's camera and, last but not least, the eyes of the trees.

**Keith Richardson**

## WAINWRIGHT'S ROWAN
### Against all the odds

*1*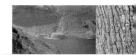

AW (1907 – 1991) was not one for making a fuss. His ashes were scattered by his wife Betty at Innominate Tarn and he certainly would not have wanted a lasting memorial in his honour in the Lakes – a sort of smaller-scale Angel of the North, heaven forbid, on his most favoured fell, Haystacks. Nor would Wainwright have wanted a mountain or a fell named after him, not to mention a plaque on a park bench. He would be content, or as content as the dear departed can ever be, to know that his unique and lovingly created Lakeland walking guides, with their hand drawn maps and images and handwritten text, have stood the test of time, are arguably more popular than ever, and show no sign, quite the contrary, of fading into oblivion. Immortality can be achieved in more ways than one.

Here, clearly, was a man who tended not to be possessive, who was not showy or greedy and, indeed, apart from an occasionally gruff exterior – surely the preserve of grumpy old men everywhere – he was generous and humble.

But there was one thing that he was happy to have "carry his name as a sort of monument." It was something that he felt quietly proud and protective of for over 30 years and was sufficiently interested in to monitor its progress at regular intervals, with a little help from his friends.

It was, intriguingly, a mountain ash or rowan tree.

And it grows to this day, against all the odds but as rowan tend to do, out of a rock face on a crag. Alfred Wainwright's affection for this particular little tree became the subject of correspondence between AW and a number of fell walkers who noted his interest in the rowan when he mentioned the tree in one of his seven volume *Pictorial Guide to the Lakeland Fells* guide books (Book Six – the North Western Fells) and in which he invited readers to write in 1970 to inform him if the tree was alive and well.

The rowan in question is situated high to one side of the steep gully of Hassnesshow Beck and it came to AW's attention in 1960 when he was pioneering a route to the summit of Robinson from Buttermere. Climbing the gully he noticed what appeared to be two twigs sticking upright from a low crag at the side of the ravine.

Wainwright's Rowan on its craggy perch above Buttermere.

Previous pages: The light show. The ancient oak woodland at Keskadale, Newlands Valley, is illuminated by sunlight slanting across the fell. The woodland has been there since late Stone Age times.

The June 1980 edition of *Cumbria* magazine published an account by AW of his find. AW wrote: "Curious, I climbed up to inspect and found to my surprise that the twigs were in fact the branches of a tiny rowan that had secured a root-hold in a thin crack in the rock face, the seed having evidently blown there or been dropped by a passing bird.

"With no visible means of sustenance, and no root run, it had nevertheless secured a firm hold. Rowans, of course, are tenacious little beggars in infancy, yet I had to admire the courage and determination of this puny specimen, surviving against all the odds. It seemed to have a message for me. Don't quit. Don't give up. Keep trying.

"I couldn't forget it. The lesson it had for me helped me on the rest of the climb. When later I described the route in the book I was writing I mentioned it. A year or two went by and letters started coming in, all assuring me that the rowan was still alive and flourishing. Since then I have had a great many reports about the state of the tree, and even a poem, from readers all over the country and from their accompanying photographs I have watched it grow in stature over the past 20 years. 1970, ten years on, brought a sheaf of correspondence. A party from Whitehaven wrote a saga of their visit, illustrated by camera studies and graphic drawings.

Tommy Orr's drawing. He sent it to AW in February 1970.

Robinson 8

ASCENT FROM HASSNESS
1900 feet of ascent : 1½ miles

A young rowan has secured a precarious roothold on this crag and was visited by a group of intrepid Alpinists on :- Monday Feb. 16th 1970.

We are pleased to be able to say that both the rowan and all our party are still alive and well.

Yours very truly,

All in c/o
T. Orr
51 Coronation Dr,
Whitehaven,
Cumberland.

W T Woodend
Gillian Dixon
George Wilson
Audrey Orr
Tommy Orr

"More years passed, never without several assurances that all was well, and I was mighty pleased to learn that the rowan was now bearing berries and developing quickly.

"On New Year's Day, 1980, the Whitehaven party made another pilgrimage, braving the snow and ice, to confirm its continuing survival, and again supplied photographs and more dramatic pen and ink illustrations of their arduous ascent.

"No single feature I have mentioned in my books has brought me more letters, not even Jack's Rake, and they have given me great pleasure. The rowan isn't my tree, but I have developed a proprietary interest in it and think of it as mine. It will outlive me and carry my name as a sort of monument. I could not wish for a better.

"Some day I will struggle up there again and renew an acquaintance that, with its message, has never been far from my mind since I noticed it in 1960."

One of the people who wrote to AW in 1970 with an update on the progress of the rowan was a member of the aforementioned Whitehaven party, Tommy Orr, who now lives in Moor Row with his wife Audrey. In fact, Tommy sent AW a drawing (see illustrations).

Tommy Orr's drawing of January 1980 depicting his group's second expedition to check on Wainwright's Rowan.

From his home at 38 Kendal Green and in correspondence dated 7th March, 1970, AW replied as follows:

*Dear Mr Orr (Tommy),*

> *I was absolutely delighted to receive your confirmation that the young rowan on the way up Robinson from Hassness is still alive and well. Indeed it is flourishing exceedingly, judging by the photographs you were kind enough to send along with your amusing illustrated report. The last time I saw it, in 1963, 'twas but a tiny two-branched sprig. From time to time, since then, I have been kept aware of its progress by other walkers who have passed that way, but yours is the first notification in 1970 and the first photographic evidence that has been supplied. The presentation of your report shows commendable initiative and talent, and I shall treasure it. Clearly the weather conditions were such that only the most intrepid of alpinists would venture forth on those cruel slopes of snow, and the whole party is to be congratulated on a performance that can surely seldom have been bettered. I have a new respect for the inhabitants of Whitehaven and especially its females.*

*Write again in 1980 and tell me the rowan is still there. Please!*

*Yours sincerely, with many thanks,*

*A Wainwright*

Tommy Orr's third drawing of January 1990.

Robinson 8

ASCENT FROM HASSNESS

579 metres of ascent : 2.4 kilometres

Once again, braving all natural & man-made hazards the band of intrepid Alpinists reached the young rowan on Monday Jan 1st 1990

"Still very much alive"

The letter, which Tommy still treasures together with another, was signed in AW's trademark signature. Ten years on in 1980 Tommy sent another drawing and information to AW and received the following reply, dated 26th January, 1980, from AW at 38 Kendal Green:

Rowan tree on the slopes of Catbells.

*Dear Mr Orr,*

*Thank you, thank you, thank you for the graphic account of your New Year's Day pilgrimage and the accompanying photographs and nail biting illustrations. What fortitude, what courage your party displayed in their determination to confirm the survival of my rowan! Congratulations to all, and especially the ageing cripples.*

*I am so touched by your devotion to the cause that I have sent off to the Editor of 'Cumbria' the 20-year saga of the rowan with two of your photos, '1970' and '1980', and demanded that he publishes it.*

*If any of your party are capable of submitting a report in 1990, please do so. I may have gone to the happy hunting grounds by then. But the rowan will still be there, bless it.*

*Yours gratefully,*
*A Wainwright.*

In 1990, Tommy Orr sent AW a third drawing but does not appear to have received a reply. Perhaps AW's health was already failing. AW died in 1991. The little rowan, with which he felt such great affinity, lives on. And it is to this day Wainwright's rowan.

While the rowan's speciality act is putting down roots in the most inhospitable locations such as crags on Lakeland fells or overhanging waterfalls in out of the way places,

The actual letter that AW sent
to Tommy Orr in January 1980.

Straight out of the fell side.
A rowan at Newlands.

there is a great deal more to this tree than meets the eye. And it all goes back to our ancestors, the Norse people who, many, many hundreds of years ago inhabited this wonderful land as settlers and moved inland from the coast and became the first fell farmers.

The name rowan comes from raun or rogn, the old Norse for the tree. The rowan is prominent in Norse mythology as the tree from which the first woman was created. The rowan is also said to have magical powers and can guard against witchcraft or evil spirits. Pieces of the tree were carried for personal protection and sprigs were used, attached to barn doors perhaps, to prevent cows and / or their dairy products from enchantment.

The rowan to be found growing out of a cleft in a rock or the trunks or boughs of other trees are the bearers of even more powerful magic and are known as 'flying rowan.' The wood of the rowan is eminently suitable for walking sticks and apparently carries added protection for late night journeys. Magicians' and Druids' staffs are also made from the rowan.

That's not all. The rowan can even embolden you and open the doorway to receiving messages from the Otherworld and spirit helpers and guides. The rowan is undoubtedly my kind of tree and there is something about it that goes far beyond appreciation of its outward beauty. I have always liked the look of the rowan with its crop of bright red berries. There are two rowan trees in my garden, one to the front and one to the back, and I hope I am doubly blessed.

# PATRIARCH OF YEW TREES
## A bike ride into history

*2*

It is a sunny afternoon in mid June and I decide on a whim to get on my bike to go and see the yew trees at Borrowdale and at Lorton. It would have been easier to whiz up the valley and over to Lorton in a car but when visiting ancient trees it seems more appropriate to use a less speedy means of transport; one that takes a lot longer and enables you to fully appreciate the journey. From behind the wheel of a fast-moving car the hedgerow is barely noticeable, from the seat of a bike it springs to life. Not only that, taking on the hills of Honister on the outward trip and Whinlatter on the homeward, tells you precisely why the bicycle is often referred to as a 'push bike.'

The trees that I am going to see have been on this planet for thousands of years, an eternity compared with the six hours or so it takes me to visit them.

It is a brilliant bike ride, and in the early stages is heading in the same direction as my favourite walk; the walk that takes me from my front door to Bar 26 on Lake Road via Walla Crag, Watendlath, Rosthwaite, the River Derwent, Grange in Borrowdale and then along the shore of Derwentwater to Hawes End landing stage and, from there, back to Keswick on a launch (see Derwentwater Scots pine, chapter 10).

The cycle route takes me out of Keswick on the Borrowdale Road and up the valley, along the shore of Derwentwater, past Lodore Falls, beneath Shepherd's Crag, beyond picturesque Grange in Borrowdale, through Rosthwaite and then sharp left to Seathwaite at the turning just before the road starts to climb perilously out of Seatoller up and over Honister. Just beyond the road branching off to Stonethwaite I am intrigued when I appear to be on the receiving end of a wolf whistle coming from a nearby garden. I stop the bike, get off and back track and, peering over the garden wall, am amused to discover that my admirer is a parrot in a cage. The parrot, clearly, has immaculate taste but I suspect it whistles at every passing cyclist or foot soldier.

The Borrowdale yews are best reached by entering the farmyard at Seathwaite and going along the path that cuts through the farm buildings to the right, crossing a wooden footbridge over the Derwent and then walking back parallel to the approach road. You will see the trees in a small grove a short distance up the fell from the beck.

Battered and bruised. One of the yew trees at Seathwaite, Borrowdale.

The grove of Borrowdale yews.

One very handsome tree, entirely separate from the main group, has its feet in the stones of the Derwent. A sign, just before you enter the fenced-off grove over a stile, reads: 'The Fraternal Four Borrowdale yews (500AD - 2005AD).' The very fact that there is a closure date of 2005AD signals immediately that the four are no more. In fact there have not been four yews here since the mid 19th Century. William Wordsworth visited the grove in 1803 and penned his poem *Yew Trees*, part of which reads:

> *But worthier still of note*
> *Are those fraternal four of Borrowdale,*
> *Joined in one solemn and capacious grove;*
> *Huge trunks! – and each particular trunk a growth*
> *Of intertwisted fibres serpentine . . .*

Eight decades after Wordsworth's visit one of the fraternal four was destroyed by a storm in 1883 and where there were four there were three. Nowadays it is more accurate to say that the three have been reduced to a rather sad looking two and a bit. The 'bit' in question is the remains of what was arguably the most spectacular of the yews in the grove. This particular tree, which once resembled a small rock face on one side – such was the solidity, width and grandeur of its stature – lost its entire crown during a storm on the night of January 5th, 2005 and all that now stands is the bleached remains of the trunk, riven and stark, a beached white whale looking very much the worse for wear. There are signs of new growth on one side of the yew but this once grand tree is now a sad spectacle, forlorn and perhaps on the way out. There are those who maintain that the yew will recover if left undisturbed, that new growth will appear over time and that a new canopy will develop. I sincerely hope so. But looking at it now I am less optimistic, even taking into account the yew's propensity for survival and longevity. In fact the entire grove has a solemn air to it, as Wordsworth acknowledged in his choice of words in the poem ('Joined in one solemn and capacious grove'). I would liken it to an elephant's graveyard with the long-dead white / grey branches resembling ivory.

The grove is overgrown with extensive bracken, scrub and bramble out of which

spring the occasional rowan, wild rose and silver birch. Murderous midges turn note taking into an endurance test and I eventually flee, pausing only to look again at the information board at the stile where a time line has been drawn between the

growth of the trees and events in history. It tells us: 500 AD, seedling years; 750 Book of Kells, Vikings attack Jarrow; 1000 (tree an adult), St Brices Day massacre; 1200, China manufactures first guns; 1500, world population reaches 400 million; 1750, Johan Sebastian Bach dies; 2000 (tree a veteran); 2005, crown destroyed.

It could go on to read: June 2010, writer does not attempt to ride up Honister Pass on bicycle. Only Tour de France riders with a million gears should attempt to scale Honister without dismounting. I didn't even make a token attempt but got off the bike and starting walking and pushing my bike at the first sight of the 25-degree slope. Walking up the pass towards the slate quarry at the summit reminds me of the

times when my father, Tommy, would walk up this road on cold winter mornings with his workmates when the surface was too icy or snowbound for the works wagon out of Keswick to make the trip. They had to break the ice on the water troughs at the works before starting work and after a hard day's toil would slip and slither their way back down in the fading light to the wagon waiting at Seatoller. My dad and his mate, John Taylor, worked at Honister until they both retired at the age of 72.

Those harsh winter work days are a far cry as I make my way up the hill, pausing occasionally for a breather in the heat. Looking down into Hause Gill, a man chops wood while his young daughters play and swim noisily in one of the clear little pools that make ideal bathing places on hot summer afternoons; once you are 'in' and have got over the initial coolness of water straight off the fell.

Honister is much changed now and is a busy tourist attraction as well as a thriving rural industry. At the apex of the climb before the sharp descent towards Buttermere I pause on the grass verge near the YHA building and am immediately accosted by four brightly plumaged cockerels scratching for food. This journey to see trees is rapidly turning into an ornithological tour.  Parrots, cockerels, whatever next?

I get on the bike and ride briefly around the Honister building with its wonderful old sign that reads: 'The Buttermere and Westmorland Green Slate Co Ltd.' Near shale heaps there is a cluster of more prominent stones that look like headstones in a graveyard, Honister's very own Boot Hill.

The brakes on the bike scream for mercy as I make the descent from Honister to Buttermere. Giant boulders dot the lower fell on either side and there are signs that bracken has been harvested from the slopes above Gatesgarthdale Beck. In the car park near to Gatesgarth Farm, a youth, John Richardson, is selling food, ice cream and drinks from a mobile van. John's great uncle was the late Johnny Richardson, once

Seatoller buildings at the foot of Honister Pass.

Honister Pass and the descent towards Buttermere.

Like glass. Buttermere.

of Gatesgarth, huntsman for the Blencathra Foxhounds and who escaped three times from German prisoner of war camps in Italy during World War 2.

The bike ride past Buttermere and Crummock Water is serene in the early evening sunshine and barnacle geese and their chicks look content on the shore at Crummock. It seems to take an eternity to reach Lorton and, weary and thirsty, I ride beyond my turn-off to High Lorton for a much needed thirst-quencher at The Wheatsheaf Inn at Low Lorton. Then I'm back on the bike, retracing my route to High Lorton and the small fenced-off yew tree on the green at a crossroads. This is the Millennium Yew planted in October 2004 and grown from a cutting taken from the famous Lorton yew just up the road. It's got a long way to go, but the sapling is showing signs of becoming a healthy and long-lived yew.

It is incredible to think that 12 Cromwellian soldiers – there to keep the peace – were among the large crowd that gathered for a Quaker meeting beneath and among the branches of the well known yew tree at Lorton, on the western fringes of the Lake District, in 1653. The celebrated Quaker George Fox, in his journal, first published in 1694, refers to the meeting at Lorton. As a young man of 28 years Fox preached at a number of meetings in Cumberland – notably in the Quaker stronghold of Swarthmoor – and was arrested for blasphemy and imprisoned in Carlisle gaol.

At a time when Quakers were persecuted there were those who wanted Fox executed. Cromwell, however, was a sympathiser and Parliament requested his release rather than have a young man die for religion. Today, as you look along the street in the village of High Lorton to the upper branches of the yew tree above the rooftops and then get as close as you can to the base of the tree itself – the yew is on private land beyond an information board – you cannot help but try and picture the scene. As many as a thousand people would attend Quaker meetings during the period when this alternative religion was in its formative stage and its leaders, especially Fox, were persecuted by the establishment. At High Lorton, many in the crowd found space and a vantage point in the branches of the yew tree itself. So much so that Fox feared for the tree's safety.

He wrote in his journal: "Now I was moved to send James Lancaster to appoint a meeting at John Wilkinson's steeplehouse near Cockermouth, who was a preacher in great repute, and had three parishes under him; wherefore I stayed in Millom-in-Bootle till he came back again. In the meantime some of those called the gentry of the country had formed a plot against me, and had given a little boy a rapier, to do

The road leading into High Lorton. The top branches of the Lorton Yew can be seen to the left of the picture.

The Lorton Yew.

me mischief with it. They came with the boy to Joseph Nicholson's house to seek me; but the Lord had so ordered it that I was gone into the fields. They met with James Lancaster but did not much abuse him; and not finding me in the house, after a while they went away again. So I walked up and down in the fields that night, and did not go to bed as very often as I used to.

"The next day we came to the steeplehouse where James Lancaster had appointed the meeting. There were at this meeting 12 soldiers and their wives, who were come thither from Carlisle; and the country people came in, as if it had been to a fair. I lay at a house a short distance from the place so that many Friends were there before me. When I came I found James Lancaster speaking under a yew tree; which was so full of people that I feared they would break it down . . ."

Fox goes on to explain that, unable to find anywhere to speak in the open, he was invited to speak in the local church and duly did so: "When the people were settled, I stood up on a seat; and the Lord opened my mouth to declare his everlasting truth."

Quakers were not the only ones to choose the Lorton yew as a venue for meetings. John Wesley, the evangelist, also spoke beneath its boughs. He preached three times in Lorton, in 1752, 1759 and 1761 and there is a small chapel in the village, built in 1840, in his memory. Other celebrity visitors – 150 years on from George Fox – were William Wordsworth and his sister Dorothy who stood under its branches in 1804.

"The next day William and I set off on our tour," wrote Dorothy. "We passed over the mountains of Whinlatter along the Cockermouth road, and through the Vale of Lorton and by Loweswater to Ennerdale. We dropped down soon after into the fertile Vale of Lorton, and went to visit a Yew tree which is the Patriarch of Yew trees, green and flourishing, in very old age – the largest yew tree I ever saw. We have many large ones in this Country but I have never seen one that would not be but a branch of this."

The stature of the Lorton yew is today considerably less than it was at the time of the visit by William and Dorothy Wordsworth. In those days it was quite a whopper – not a description employed by Wordsworth, more's the pity – and in 1794 its spread was 20 metres, right across the nearby Whit Beck and almost to the road. In fact it is probably now only a third of its original maximum size. The reasons that it is much diminished are a combination of storms, limbs dying and what amounted – viewed from the 21st Century – to legalised vandalism in that its branches were lopped off to make weavers' shuttles. Not long after Wordsworth wrote his poem the 27-foot trunk was reduced by storm to 13 feet in diameter and some of the wood was fashioned into chairs, one of which is a mayoral seat still used in Cockermouth.

The tree has also survived attempts to cut it down in its entirety and at one point it was described, rather cruelly, as a ruin. Personally, I think it now looks composed and the streamlined version is probably better equipped to withstand the onslaught of a tempest and to add considerably to its reputed 1,400 years of life.

The Lorton yew stands on the side of the rushing burble that is Whit Beck, directly opposite the original Jennings Brewery malt house – the first Jennings ales were brewed at Lorton in 1828 – and just down the way from a small bridge, Boonbeck Bridge, that is full of character. The old malt house still has the outward appearance of a mill building and I can imagine the brewery workers taking a well-earned break on the banks of the stream. In a possibly romanticised image I like to think of them lolling around on the bank of the beck in the midday sunshine, eating bread and cheese and supping beer and perhaps dangling a rod and line in the water for trout.

The tree is in a sheltered position but at one time it would have stood on its own alongside the nearby Boon Beck Farm, long before the mill building and other early High Lorton properties appeared on the scene; including the wonderful brewery cottages, one of which has the name Yan Yak (one oak), with their quaint outside flights of steps. My latest visit to the tree on a warm summer's evening was thoroughly pleasant. The tree itself looked in the peak of condition. It is situated on fenced off land right next to Whit Beck and close to the rear of the old malting house, now the village hall. A plaque at the entrance to the hall announces in vibrant gold lettering on a background of Lakeland slate that the village hall is actually called 'The Yew Tree Hall' and that in 1910 Jennings gifted the building to the community and trustees when the brewery moved to its current home in Cockermouth.

I had a good feeling about the yew tree at Lorton. People have a tendency to give trees 'human' traits and that is perhaps unfortunate. Trees do have distinctive

characters and if you want to touch or talk to them then fine; just don't expect them to answer back unless, that is, the higher branches and foliage whisper to you on the wind.

The yew tree at Lorton appeared to be very well looked after, was in good shape and beneath its boughs were a couple of pieces of agricultural machinery. All looked tidy and in its place. Even a small trampoline, a child's plaything in this garden of Eden, with its magnificent views across the fields to the fells, did not seem entirely out of place. In fact there is something apt about a child playing near a tree reputedly 1,400 years old. Sunlight played on the lower trunk where logs for the winter fire had been stacked. Roofing slates had been leant against the wall skirting the beck and, without trespassing onto the garden in which the tree stands, it was possible for me to follow the beck round, below and on the outside of the low wall, and there get a close up view of the tree. Sawn off limbs of branches sat to one side of its base.

The visit in 1804 was not the only one by William Wordsworth to the yew at Lorton. William Musgrave, of Lorton, and Wordsworth were boyhood friends when the latter was living in Cockermouth.

On one occasion when William visited the yew he fell in the beck under the tree, and had to be sent back to Cockermouth in some of Musgrave's clothes. He was obviously fond of the yew and those at Borrowdale (those fraternal four) and his poem *Yew Trees*, written in 1803, was the result:

*There is a Yew-tree, pride of Lorton Vale*

*Which to this day stands single, in the midst*

*Of its own darkness, as it stood of yore,*

*Not loth to furnish weapons for the Bands*

*Of Umfraville or Percy ere they marched*

*To Scotland's Heaths; or Those that crossed the Sea*

*And drew their sounding bows at Azincour,*

*Perhaps at early Crecy, or Poictiers.*

*Of vast circumference and gloom profound*

*This solitary tree! – a living thing*

*Produced too slowly ever to decay;*

*Of form and aspect too magnificent*

*To be destroyed. But worthier still of note*

*Are those fraternal four of Borrowdale,*

*Joined in one solemn and capacious grove;*

*Huge trunks! – and each particular trunk a growth*

*Of intertwisted fibres serpentine*

*Up coiling, and inveterately convolved, –*

*Nor uniformed with Phantasy, and looks*

*That threaten the prophane; – a pillared shade,*

*Upon whose grassless floor of red-brown hue,*

*By sheddings from the pining umbrage tinged*

*Perenially – beneath whose sable roof*

*Of boughs, as if for festal purpose, decked*

*With unrejoicing berries, ghostly Shapes*

*May meet at noontide; Fear and trembling Hope,*

*Silence and Foresight; Death the Skeleton*

*And Time the Shadow; – there to celebrate.*

*As in a natural temple scattered o'er*

*With altars undisturbed of mossy stone,*

*United worship; or in mute repose*

*To lie, and listen to the mountain flood*

*Murmuring from Glaramara's inmost caves.*

## MARTINDALE YEW
### Another world

*3*

To enter The Old Church of St Martin in remote and semi-secluded Martindale is to walk into another world. The church dates back more than 700 years and to step inside this ancient building – in 1266 it was known as The Chapel of St Martin – is to feel as though you have been sucked clean out of 21st Century Lakeland, and propelled back in time to a black and white universe where the parameters between right and wrong are self-evident, religion is key and God is in his heaven. The internal décor and design of the church is so minimalist and basic that you could readily imagine a frock-coated preacher spouting goblets of hellfire and damnation at his God-fearing flock.

Despite the spartan furniture (the pulpit bears the date 1634) 17th Century flagged stone floor and double rows of pews that line the walls beneath leaded windows and wooden-arched ceiling, the atmosphere in the church is anything but cold and gloomy. In fact it is friendly and welcoming. In a world where money rules more than ever, commercialism is rampant and appears to be our only true god, the austerity and simplicity of this building has a feel-good factor that draws you in and makes you want to linger and absorb the peace and the silence, broken only by the soft rush of the wind in the branches of the yew outside, the bleat of a lamb or the raucous caw of a rook.

Who knows, you might even hear voices and / or receive a sign to a higher calling when you are least expecting it. Imagine the scenario. So there I was . . . I popped into the church for a look-see while on a visit to the yew tree in the churchyard and, hey presto, I'm now on the evangelical trail, my life has changed forever, and 'Billy' Graham's my hero.

The only religious experience of any note that I can recall happened when I was young boy and taken to a meeting in the Skiddaw Street convention tent, home of the world famous annual religious convention in Keswick. Listening to one of the speakers I was overcome by a sense of purity and determined that I would do good, as in religious good, for the rest of my days. It lasted for about four days, possibly less; okay maybe for a night. But I was young and very impressionable.

Martindale in swirling mist.

Any chances that the peace and quiet of Martindale might lead to a belated form of divine intervention were shattered when a small cluster of children, I think there were three, burst noisily into the church accompanied by a woman who I assumed was their mum. The silence and reverie were instantly broken and to add to the volume the voice of Katherine Jenkins and accompanying orchestra was belting out *I Believe*, courtesy of mum's iPlayer. If this was God's way of telling me that it wasn't too late for me to change my ways then I'm afraid I wasn't listening. I headed outside for the greater solitude – rooks apart – of the branches of the yew I had come to see in the first place, leaving behind the strains of *I Believe* and its intrinsic message of hope for a better world in which children laugh, war has been banned and people of all creeds and colours share words of love and devotion, stand up and feel the Holy Spirit, find the power of faith and open their hearts. 'Yes, I believe,' as the lyrics of the song say.

It is believed that the yew in the churchyard at St Martin's is about 1,300 years old and, in common with many more yew trees throughout Cumbria and the Lake District, pre dates the churchyard in which it is located. The famous bowmen of Martindale made their bows from its branches and yeoman archers were a deadly

force on foreign fields as 500 of them alone could rain down over 5,000 arrows a minute on the heads of the French at 14th Century killing fields such as Poitiers and Agincourt.

The knowledge that the wood from this self same yew, situated in a sacred and peaceful grove deep in the Cumbrian fells, was responsible for death and mayhem in 14th Century France, is hard to comprehend. But it happened.

Taking the path alongside the church, beyond the longish grass and tired-looking daffodils, I opened the lowering branches of the yew like a curtain and walked into an open space where the trunk of the ancient yew stands proud and the branches reach out and touch the ground. Someone had placed a bunch of daffodils on the lower part of the trunk. Perhaps the pagans are back, returning to their ancient sacred place where their ancestors worshipped at this site long before the arrival of the Christian church.

The circle was very important to our ancestors, hence the stone circle and the use of circle or spiral designs on stones. The circle is also significant in terms of the yew tree. Drooping branches touch the ground in circular formation and are 'reborn'

The minimalist interior of the
Old Church of St Martin.

with new life springing up and new trees formed from the parent. Similarly, the main trunk of an older tree becomes hollow and the tree begins to grow fresh wood from the inside. I once stepped inside the main yew at Borrowdale, before it was badly damaged by a storm, and stared directly up through the trunk at the sky.

Our modern take on yew trees in graveyards is one of death. However, for our ancestors the yew tree was a symbol of immortality and rebirth. It was a holy tree, a tree of life. Having said that the yew – with the exception of the flesh of its little red berries – is highly poisonous and can kill. It is the longest-lived species of tree in the northern hemisphere and its wood is reputed to last longer than iron.

Unlike the interior of the small church it is eerie beneath the yew at Martindale, the doom-laden atmosphere enhanced by the mournful caw of the rooks above, reluctant to leave the nest or be disturbed by occasional visitors. To make matters even more otherworldly, a sombre tomb (is there such a thing as happy tomb?) stands on the loose stones and soil, exposed roots, broken twigs and autumnal debris directly beneath the yew. At the time of my visit, in early May, it is impossible to make out the epitaph

engraved on its surface because it has been splattered extensively by droppings from the rooks that have made their nests in the upper branches of the yew.

This, however, is not the tomb of one Richard Birkett who became the first vicar of St Martin's in 1633 on a stipend of £6 13s 4d a year. His tomb is situated elsewhere in the churchyard where his epitaph reads: 'Here lieth interred Richard Birkett clerk who procured this chappell to be consecrated with parochial rights. As curat he remained here 67 years. And as a benefactor he gave ye chappell one hundred pounds. As a most affectionate husband he left to his wife a comfortable subsistence who in token of her gratitude and to perpetuate his memory caused this tomb to be erected. He died on the 25th of December in the 95th year of his age. Anno Domini 1699.'

Prior to Richard Birkett's arrival and until the Dissolution of the Monasteries in 1536, the monks of Barton served the Chapelry of Martindale and it remained part of the parish of Barton until 1633.

The history of the church is also linked to Roman times. It is dedicated to St Martin, apparently a Roman soldier who converted to Christianity. The church contains a Roman artefact in that the font is originally believed to have been a Roman altar brought down, perhaps 500 years ago, from the Roman road on High Street at the head of the dale. This stone was used on the fell to sharpen agricultural tools and deep scratch marks are to be seen on its surface.

St Martin's is still used regularly with services once a month but in the late 19th Century it was usurped, for want of a better word, by a bigger church developed just round the corner and on top of the hill, known as Hallin Hause and overlooking Ullswater. This is The New Church of St Peter and – read into this what you will – on the day that the new church was consecrated on January 6th, 1882, the roof of the old church was destroyed during a storm.

Before the arrival of the children, their mother, *I Believe* and the orchestra, I took the opportunity to stand at the reading desk or pulpit (dated 1634) in St Martin's, open the Bible to a page at

random and cast my eyes over the print, hoping that something might strike a chord. I turned to Psalms 42 – 44 and the words that attracted my attention were: 'Yet you have rejected and humbled us and no longer lead our armies into battle. You have forced us to retreat before the foe, and our enemies have plundered us at will. You have given us up to be slaughtered like sheep and scattered us among the nations . . .'

It is spring in Lakeland and from the fell outside the church comes the sound of a lamb bleating for its mother. This is a land of fell walkers, knapsacks, walking poles and shepherds on quad bikes. But if you linger long enough it will be rent asunder by the scream and the roar of low flying jets tearing down and across the valley and bringing with them the sounds that are now familiar in war zones like Afghanistan. Standing alongside the yew tree that produced an effective weapon of war in a different age you realise that only a few hundred years separate Agincourt and the modern day struggle in Afghanistan. Some things, it would appear, never change. It is only the weapons that we use that have become increasingly sophisticated, wider ranging and more deadly. We have come a long way but, in truth, have learned very little.

Images of the tomb beneath the yew at The Old Church of St Martin.

## SHAKESPEARE'S OAK
### My kingdom for an oak

4

Shakespeare's Oak on Kendal Green is no more. Well, that's not strictly true. The trunk of the tree lies in two in the grounds of the nearby St Thomas's Church of England School where it provides a unique plaything for the school children. The tree in its entirety once stood proud on the rim of the lovely area of land that is Kendal Green, a large, undulating, and more or less rectangular sward surrounded by substantial houses, some of which date back to the mid 1800s.

The Green itself in Kendal Green is an attraction in its own right and provides an area of relative calm a short distance away from the busy Windermere road that leads down House of Correction Hill – there was a prison there at one time – into a town centre that arguably boasts one of the most unforgiving one way road systems in Christendom threading this way and that over the River Kent.

On the occasions that I have visited the Green in summer the weather has always been spectacularly hot and sunny, almost Mediterranean in its intensity, but the scene that greets you is unmistakeably English and it is not difficult to imagine the immensely well supported events

Shakespeare's Oak as it was when it stood on Kendal Green. Today the trunk of the tree is in the playground of a nearby school.

that took place here in Victorian and Edwardian times; not least the planting of The Shakespeare Oak on April 25, 1864. The tree was planted to celebrate the 300th anniversary of the world famous poet and playwright's birthday, April 23, 1564.

The planting of the tree in 1864 was a very grand occasion. In their thoroughly researched and lovingly published book *Kendal Green – a Georgian Wasteland Transformed*, John and Jean Coopey, who live at No 24 Kendal Green in an Edwardian property situated directly in front of where Shakespeare's oak once stood, record that the town's schoolchildren were given a half day holiday and all tradesmen were asked to close their shops for the afternoon. *The Kendal Mercury and Northern Advertiser* reported that on the day the planting and celebration took place in Kendal similar events were being held around England, including Stratford on Avon (unsurprisingly) and in London where a working mens' demonstration took place in the city and an oak was planted on Primrose Hill. The Bishop of Dublin, preaching in St James, praised Shakespeare as a 'great gift from God.'

In Kendal at 1pm the town bells rang out and one hour later the schoolchildren gathered in the market place accompanied by the Rifle Band, Mr Wallace's Band and the Workhouse Union Drum and Fife Band.

"About 1,500 children had been assembled and proceeded," reported the *Mercury*, "with a band of music in front and another in the rear, to the Tenter Fell (on what is now Kendal Green). The children also carried a large number of flags and banners kindly supplied by Foster Braithwaite (Edwardian marketing at its best – my words, not the Mercury's) whose exertions throughout for the success of the celebration has been beyond praise of ours. The procession was now directed towards the Low Tenter Fell where a large number of people – we have heard the number on the Fell, young and old, estimated at 5,000 – soon assembled to witness the planting of the Shakespeare Oak.

"At the sound of a bugle there was silence and the mayor, in a few remarks, explained the object of planting an oak in memory of England's greatest poet.

He then introduced to the people Master John Wakefield (the Wakefields and the Braithwaites were highly regarded families of the time in Kendal) a child of about six years of age who went to work vigorously to dig the hole and plant the tree and name it 'Shakespeare's Oak' after which the Mayor hoisted the young gentleman on his shoulders and presented him to the people, amid loud cheers, as the workman of the day.

"The Mayor, then hoisting aloft a large green placard bearing the words 'Kendal Green', said that he had great pleasure in naming the plot of ground on which they were now assembled Kendal Green, by which name it would, henceforth, be known. It was part of the ground secured for the public for everlasting possession."

The children were then marched through a tent and presented with a medal, a ribbon and a bun. They also received a packet of lozenges from local grocer Mr Greenwood (aptly named and another example of Edwardian commercialism targeting youth) and there was a scramble for nuts."

The tree was subsequently railed in for protection and the Mercury hoped "it will flourish we trust for very many generations."

Kendal Green (centre right) just beyond the terrace houses (image left) and on this page from a closer perspective.

That evening a Shakespearean literary and musical entertainment was held and the good old *Mercury* reported that it was "a good old fashioned social tea where ladies could enjoy themselves as well as gentlemen, seated at tables and not standing after the new style." The entrance fee was 1s/6d and those present were given an introductory address, a eulogy to Shakespeare and the English language and were entertained by instrumentalists and vocal performances."

The reports in the *Mercury* refer to Tenter Fell and to Low Tenter Fell and this is significant. In his play Henry IV part one a character who in the original version was known as Sir John Oldcastle and in the more popular, later version, as Falstaff, refers to being allegedly attacked by "three misbegotten knaves in Kendal green." This is the name given to the rough woollen cloth made in Kendal in Shakespearean times and which was as common place then as, say, denim is today. Not only that, the place Kendal Green, where Shakespeare's Oak was planted with such amazing ceremony and with a cast of thousands in 1864, was also the location where the Kendal green cloth was hung out to stretch and dry after it was dyed its distinctive colour. The frames on which the cloth was hung were known as tenter frames and gave rise to the phrase 'on tenterhooks.'

So the Shakespearean connection with Kendal is not solely restricted to the planting of an oak in recognition of the 300th anniversary of the writer's birth. Kendal Castle, which can be glimpsed over the rooftops, enhances the historical / Shakespearean feel of the place and, as in the foremost plays by the bard, other forces are at play here.

Falstaff's reference to the Kendal green cloth clearly does not signify that the playwright actually visited the town of Kendal, although he might easily have done so at some stage, but it does give the town instant and quite unique recognition. It also makes for fascinating reading as Falstaff attempts to mask the true events of an incident in which he claims he was attacked under cover of darkness, only for his lie to be exposed by Prince Henry amid a flurry of colourful Shakespearean insults:

FALSTAFF: But, as the devil would have it, three misbegotten knaves in Kendal green came at my back and let drive at me; for it was so dark Hal, that thou couldst not see thy hand.

PRINCE HENRY: These lies are like their father that begets them – gross as a mountain, open, palpable. Why, thou clay-brained guts, thou knotty-pated fool, thou whoreson, obscene, greasy tallow-catch–

FALSTAFF: What, art thou mad? Art thou mad? Is not the truth the truth?

PRINCE HENRY: Why, how couldst thou know these men in Kendal green when it was so dark thou couldst not see thy hand? Come, tell us your reason: what say'st thou to this?

FALSTAFF: What, upon compulsion? No. Were I at the strappado, or all the racks in the world, I would not tell you on compulsion. Give you a reason on compulsion? If reasons were as plentiful as blackberries I would give no man a reason upon compulsion, I.

PRINCE HENRY: I'll be no longer guilty of this sin. This sanguine coward, this bed-presser, this horseback-breaker, this huge hill of flesh–

FALSTAFF: Away, you starveling, you elf-skin, you dried neat's tongue, bull's pizzle, you stock-fish! O, for breath to utter what is like thee! You tailor's yard, you sheath, you bowcase, you vile standing-tuck–

PRINCE HENRY: Well, breathe awhile, and then to't again: and when thou hast tired thyself in base comparisons, hear me speak but thus . . . we two saw you four set on four and bound them, and were masters of their wealth. Mark now how a plain tale shall put you down. Then did we two set on you four, and with a word, out-faced you from your prize, and have it, yea, and can show it you in the house. And, Falstaff, you carried your guts away as nimbly, with as quick dexterity, and roared for mercy and still ran and roared, as ever I heard a bull calf. What a slave art thou, to hack thy sword as thou hast done, and then say it was in fight! What trick, what device, what starting-hole canst thou now find out to hide thee from this open and apparent shame?

Not unlike Falstaff's poor attempt to hide the truth, the Shakespeare Oak on Kendal Green was not a masterpiece among trees. This tree was not one of great beauty that would stand out in a crowd. It was, to put it bluntly, a straggly oak and other trees on Kendal Green had far greater appeal. There are quite a number of different trees on the green – horse chestnut, sycamore and lime to name a few – but the most prominent are two gigantic wellingtonia. These were probably planted to commemorate the marriage of the Prince of Wales (later King Edward VII) to Princess Alexandra of Denmark. It is perhaps significant that 53 Kendal Green, near where the wellingtonia stand, is called Denmark House and the first terrace of three houses built on the Green as early as 1864 was called Denmark Terrace. Rumour has it that treasure is buried beneath the roots of one of the wellingtonia.

Shakespeare's Oak was a veritable pauper alongside these regal companions of the tree world, but what it did have – and, indeed, still has even though its remains now reside in a nearby school playground – is a place in history and a title not to be taken lightly, the name of a man who was the world's greatest writer in the English language and who, along the way, immortalised a little piece of Cumbria and, more particularly Westmorland, through using the Kendal green cloth in one of his plays. A handsome green-painted plaque with white lettering, giving some information about Shakespeare's Oak and its connections and heritage, still stands in the wall opposite where the tree once stood.

Shakespeare's Oak was felled in 2009. Picture courtesy of John and Jean Coopey.

House of Correction Hill and the former Kendal Prison behind the high wall. Picture courtesy of the Margaret Duff Collection.

The tree came down to earth in 2009 when it was axed. In its place is now a scarlet oak which, apparently, is not vulnerable to the honey fungus that ultimately killed the original Shakespeare's Oak by attacking its roots.

Finally, I was fascinated by the name 'House of Correction Hill,' referred to in the opening paragraph of the chapter. This is on the main road leading out of Kendal, the Windermere Road, and is only a short distance from Green Road and Caroline Street (where once stood a workhouse), both of which lead onto Kendal Green. At one time, as can be seen from the image, the prison dominated the local landscape with its massive walls, factory-like structure and two big chimneys. It is very Dickensian and is in stark contrast to the sense of freedom created by the washing on the line in nearby gardens.

John and Jean Coopey's book reveals that the original prison – a more modest affair – was established under the Poor Law Acts of 1601 and 1640. It was completely rebuilt and extended in the late 1700s and the early 1800s. The description 'House of Correction' became obsolete under the Prison Act of 1877 when its title was changed to Her Majesty's Prison, Kendal. It ceased to be a civilian jail in 1894 when it became a military prison. It was sold in 1907 and subsequently knocked down and provided stone for new build in the town.

At one time prisoners were apparently permitted to use Low Tenter Fell for exercise and one gaoler let them play football. When it was time for them to return to their cells he would shout: "Now then lads, you must follow me or if you don't I'll lock you oot!" He was clearly years ahead of his time.

Tenter Fell on Kendal Green. The ridges were where the tenter frames were placed in lines.

The trunk of the oak in the school playground.

## SYCAMORE GAP
### Taking liberties

*5*

Movies made in the United States occasionally take liberties with character, dialogue, time and location. Ahem, perhaps that's an understatement. Who could possibly forget John Wayne's immaculately Yankee delivery, as the Roman Centurion at the crucifixion of Christ in *The Greatest Story Ever Told* (1965), of the words: 'Truly this man was the son of Gard'.

In *Robin Hood: Prince of Thieves* (1991) the geographical boundaries are stretched beyond snapping point when Robin (Kevin Costner) returns from The Crusades with Azeem (Morgan Freeman) only to find that his father, Lord Locksley, has been murdered (yes, the booming voice of Brian Blessed silenced) his lands claimed by the evil Sheriff of Nottingham (Alan Rickman) and the people subjected to tyranny, starvation and all manner of things that evil sheriffs tend to get up to; cue maniacal laughter, fearsome glares, underhand sword thrusts, torture in the dungeon and much taking advantage of innocent wenches, all before, during or after gorging on food and quaffing wine.

Hadrian's Wall looking towards Crag Lough and Hotbank Farm.

Painting of Sycamore Gap by Peter Phillips.
www.peterphillipsart.com

It's a fun movie, seriously, if you don't take it over seriously and one which I enjoyed. It provided further unexpected entertainment after I visited one very special film location – Sycamore Gap on Hadrian's Wall, due west of the impressive Housesteads Roman Fort – and returned home to replay the film and pay particular attention to the script and the geography. As the film is American-made you make allowances (the hell I did) and just go with it. Having said that it is intriguing to note that when Robin and Azeem make landfall in not so merry old England, after their escape from painful and prolonged incarceration in some hell hole in Jerusalem, it is from a rowing boat onto the shore below the white cliffs of Dover where Robin prostrates himself, kisses the sand and proclaims: "Thank you Lord – I'm home! I'm home!"

I appreciate that he was referring to his country, England, as opposed to town, city, county or garden gate, but, for the sake of pedantry, I always thought that the more specific home for Robin was Nottingham and Sherwood Forest and the land thereabouts. I mention this because a few minutes after arriving off Dover, Robin and Azeem are seen striding out purposefully over Hadrian's Wall which, the last time I looked at the map, was some 300 miles and the rest due north of Dover and quite a long way from Nottingham. I can only presume that they must have taken the scenic route. No matter.

This is the stage in the early frames of the movie that the wonderfully situated tree at scenic Sycamore Gap on Hadrian's Wall makes its star appearance. A joyous Robin is seen atop the wall by the tree, leaping about, swirling his cloak, emitting one or two decidedly American whoops and hollers and crying out, once more – just in case we missed the point earlier – "I'm home!" At that stage he is blissfully unaware of the fate that has befallen his father, land and people. Azeem is sticking with Robin because he has vowed to save his life after Locksley saved his in the Holy

Land. Walking along the wall they enter into a discourse about the merits of love and women, all sparked off by Robin jumping up and taking a twig and leaves from a lower branch on the Sycamore, and shouting to Azeem: "Look, mistletoe . . . the new maid lost her resolve to me thanks to this little plant." Mistletoe, for the record, does not grow in the sycamore on Hadrian's Wall, or at least it didn't when I was there. But what the heck, this is Hollywood and the white cliffs of Dover are a hop, skip and a jump from Hadrian's Wall.

Robin and Azeem continue along the wall, exchanging pleasantries about women, seduction, romantic endeavour, heartbreak and the like when Azeem is suddenly distracted and, with sunset approaching, it is clearly time for him to pray to Mecca.

"Is there no sun in this cursed country – which way is East?" He asks Robin.

Robin points to the East and when Azeem asks him if he is sure, Robin replies with great authority: "I would know blindfold, I'm five miles from home."

It would now appear that Nottingham and Sherwood Forest have been transplanted to within a marauding Pict's striking distance of Hadrian's Wall. Oh well.

Sycamore Gap.

As Azeem faces east, kneels and prays to his maker Robin hears the sound of men on horseback with hounds at their heels. He rushes to the edge of the wall, looks over and discovers that the hunt is on and the prey is a young lad who is being pursued by the Sheriff's men (for poaching the Sheriff's deer). The boy clambers into the branches of the sycamore to escape his pursuers – quite a feat as when I attempted the same I found it impossible to reach a lower branch, let alone climb into the tree. But then I wasn't being pursued by deerhounds and the sheriff's men, led by the sheriff's cousin, a nasty piece of work called Guy of Gisborne (Michael Wincott).

In the movie one of the soldiers has similar problems in attempting to scale the sycamore to bring the boy back to earth and is about to resort, instead, to chopping the tree down with an axe when Robin intercedes. The boy protests that he had to steal the meat because the Sheriff was starving the people.

"I advise you to move on pilgrim," says Guy of Gisborne through his yellow and broken teeth. "This is the Sheriff's land."

"Wrong," says Robin. "This is my land and my tree, therefore whatever's in it also belongs to me."

Guy of Gisborne: "Might I have the pleasure of your name before I have you run through."

Robin: "Robin of Locksley."

Guy of Gisborne: "Well, well . . . Locksley. Welcome home. Kill him!"

As Azeem continues to pray on the hill above, Robin fights off his attackers and, finally, has Gisborne at his mercy, sword to his throat. Robin, of course, spares the man, sends him off with a word of warning for the Sheriff of Nottingham as to his future conduct and utters the immortal words: "I've seen enough blood spilled to last two lifetimes – now get off my land!"

It is as though the dastardly Guy of Gisborne has been reduced to the status of an errant rambler who has strayed off a permitted footpath and is being remonstrated with by an angry farmer.

Whatever the liberties they took relating to time and place and dialect, the filmmakers of *Robin Hood: Prince of Thieves* cannot be criticised for selecting Hadrian's Wall and the surrounding countryside as a location. It is epic. And the area around

Sycamore Gap is spectacular with the sycamore itself sitting comfortably at the base of a U in the land and the roll of the wall. All around are big Northumbrian skies, space and countryside that seem to go on forever. The defiant character of the wall itself and, at this point, the daunting cliffs of the Whin Sill ridge and the beauty of Crag Lough – complete with a pair of mating swans – all combine to make this a very special place where history is defined by the scale of the wall and its milecastles and forts as it snakes across the country. The views are sensational.

Hadrian's Wall protected the most northerly frontier of the Roman Empire. The emperor Hadrian decided on its construction in 122AD. The wall, which took 15 years to build, was 80 miles long and stretched from Wallsend near Newcastle in the east to Bowness on Solway on the Cumbrian coast to the west. There were 13 forts along its length, of which the ruins at Housesteads are the finest remaining example. The wall's garrison of several thousand men was drawn from all over the Roman Empire, from Germany and Belgium to Romania and Bulgaria.

I walked out along the wall to the west on a circular route from Housesteads through Housesteads Wood, over Cuddy's Crags, Highshield Crags (with Crag Lough below), Sycamore Gap, and Peel Crags to Steel Rigg where a path brings you back round on the other side of the lough along Peatrigg and through Hotbank Farm to rejoin the outward path. Returning to Housesteads I spent an hour or so walking around the remains of the fort. During the walk along the wall I met a number of Americans and Canadians – part of a tour that had arrived at the wall that day – and the fort itself was busy with tourists. There appeared to be a lot of interest in the Roman latrines at Housesteads where a helpful drawing on the signage shows a row of soldiers using this communal facility that reminded me, in part, of the wooden outside loo we used in my childhood home at Low Briery on the outskirts of Keswick. While we had separate units for privacy, the round hole in the wooden surface of the toilet was much the same as its Roman prototype.

On the other hand, our hot bath was most definitely not as sophisticated as the Romans'. It consisted of a tin bath of painfully hot water in front of the fire or, if you were small and young enough, a scrub down as you stood, naked to the world, in the kitchen sink. Those were the days.

## THE REBEL TREE
### The last battle on English soil

6

Visiting the site of a long-ago battle you find yourself imagining the confrontation between the warring factions, the cries, the screams, the drums, the sound of cavalry and foot soldiers on the move, the blood, the bravery, the raw fear, the wounded, the dead and the dying. Research through archives, books, newspapers and various documents – first hand accounts of those who fought or were bystanders – all helps to build a picture. As you roam over the terrain of the battlefield, invariably in the rain, you pay particular attention to characteristics of the land or to buildings that stood at the time. And you endeavour to subtract all the influences of 21st Century society and developments – railway lines and motorways, hotels, schools and houses – that throw a disguise over, in this case, events at Clifton Moor in the fading light of a cold afternoon on Wednesday, December 18, 1745 when the Jacobites and the Government's Hanoverian forces clashed in what is reputed to be the last battle fought on English soil.

I say reputed because some historians will argue that it was not a battle (dictionary definition 'a prolonged fight between large organised armed forces') but only a skirmish ('a piece of irregular or unpremeditated fighting between smaller or outlying parts of the armies'). Either way I am in no doubt that it was a bloody battle for those who took part and especially those whose heads were split asunder by broadsword, ribs splintered by musket bullet and whose bones still rest in the soil of Clifton, beneath an oak tree known as The Rebel Tree in the case of the Jacobites and in a communal grave at St Cuthbert's Church, where the remains of Hanoverian government soldiers are buried. Figures vary as to how many were killed and wounded at Clifton and, as in modern warfare, both sides claimed victory. Some things never change.

In death, as in life, those who were killed at Clifton are set marginally apart – the Government troops in a churchyard, the Jacobites beneath a tree a few hundred yards up the road – but now they share for all eternity the rich earth of the Eden Valley where they fought and died.

The Rebel Tree – which I first heard about in casual conversation – is an oak

The Rebel Tree at Clifton.

situated along a dirt track, adjacent to new buildings known as Town End Croft, near The George and Dragon public house / restaurant in Clifton. As oaks go it is a solid specimen with a twisted lower trunk. But it has the distinction of being something of a shrine to the Jacobite movement and a memorial to the warriors, thought to be 12 but possibly as few as five (records, such as they are, vary) buried beneath its branches.

A solitary standing stone – a memorial to the Jacobites – was partly covered by a heavy fallen bough and I had to clear a path, as best I could, to see the epitaph at close quarters. It was difficult to make out in the gloom of a grey, sodden late afternoon but the words on the stone are: 'Here lie buried the men of the army of Prince Charles who fell at Clifton Moor 18 December 1745'. On the gate at the entrance to the small, enclosed area where the Jacobites are buried is a plaque that reads:

*In Memory*
*Of Fellow Scots Who Lie Here on Foreign Soil*
*Never Forgotten*
*Prosperity to Scotland And No Union*
*Soil nan Gaidheal**

Another plaque at the grave reads: 'In memory of those members of Prince Charles Edward Stuart's Jacobite forces who fell in action at Clifton 18th December 1745. Their sacrifice for the cause of the true king is not forgotten.' These words are attributed to The Fifteen, The Northumbrian Jacobite Society.

Nearby are other symbols of remembrance, the remains of a wreath, a white cockade (symbol of the uprising and worn by Jacobite fighters and supporters) and a key ring bearing an image of William Wallace, 1661 / 1720, and inscribed 'William Wallace the Scot, terror of the enemies.' There is also a rough wooden plaque, attached to the enclosure fence, with the name 'Buchanan' writ large on its surface. The shredded corners of a Scots flag can be seen where the Saltire was once nailed to the same fence, most probably on December 17, 2006, when a group of 25 supporters of Crann Tara* travelled from Scotland to Clifton. In full Scottish regalia, pipes and bearing flags, they marched through the village to rededicate the site; Jacobites, on the march south once more, to reclaim their throne.

The battle / skirmish, call it what you will, of Clifton Moor followed the retreat of Bonnie Prince Charles' Jacobite army from Derby where his military campaign deep into English territory ground to a halt – a lack of support from English Jacobites was at the heart of the arguably ill-fated decision to retreat – with London and the crown within striking distance. It was the Prince's counsel of leaders – acting in part on misleading information proffered by a spy – that took the decision to retreat north. Prince Charles himself was for pushing on regardless and his demeanour and body language during the retreat spoke volumes about his feelings.

Instead of being to the fore as he was on the way south – triumphantly entering Carlisle on the back of a white charger with a 100 pipers serenading his victory in taking the Border city and castle – he rode to the rear of the main body of his retreating army and cut an increasingly unhappy figure. It could also be argued that his subsequent decision-making was flawed, not least at Culloden. What would have happened had the Prince and his army continued to fight their way towards London? We will never know; speculation never won or lost a battle.

The entire sequence of events began when William III of Orange deposed Prince Charles' grandfather, James II and VII of Scotland, who had ruled from 1685 – 1689. Following the exile of James II the Jacobite cause strove to overthrow the reigning House of Hanover and restore the House of Stuart as rulers of England and Scotland. Prince Charles was the big white hope, but it all eventually came to a bloody end at Culloden on April 16, 1746, when the army of William Augustus, Duke of Cumberland, defeated the Jacobite army. Not content with that the duke, his officers and troops, then embarked on an 18th Century equivalent of ethnic cleansing in the Highlands. Known as the 'pacification' of Jacobite areas, pacify in this instance meant to kill not only rebels, but also non-combatant sympathisers, burn their houses and confiscate livestock. Those who survived the revenge of the redcoats starved to death the next winter. The obese Duke of Cumberland, while apparently popular with his soldiers, was known as 'Butcher' and the Highlands flowed with blood and with tears.

The events at Clifton in mid December 1745 were clearly just one part of the conflict between the warring parties as the Jacobite Rising rose, unfolded and fell, losing impetus en route to its final fatal encounter at Culloden and the bloody repercussions of instant justice or, for those taken alive, long periods of incarceration in squalid conditions, trial and transportation or execution; the latter being the brutal hung, drawn and quartered.

The events at Clifton occurred over a few hours of near darkness as the light faded late on a cold winter's day and the moon, darting out of the clouds, offered flashes of illumination. Various first hand accounts exist of the clash at Clifton between the retreating Jacobites and the pursuing forces of The Duke of Cumberland. One of the combatants on the side of Bonnie Prince Charlie was the Chevalier de Johnstone, the son of an Edinburgh merchant, well connected to some of the best Scottish families, and who liked to live life to the full. In modern day parlance he was a party animal. He was sent by the family to live with two uncles in Russia in the hope that he might mature and return a much-changed young man. Unfortunately for the family, but not necessarily for himself or those in his social whirl, he was as amiable and as dissolute as before and possibly more so, making up for lost time.

While his character was all embracing in its pursuit of pleasure the young man had been educated in firm Episcopalian and Jacobite principles and when Bonnie Prince Charlie set foot on these shores, the Chevalier de Johnstone was one of the first to join the cause. He was appointed aide-de-camp to Lord George Murray and, for a short time, assistant aide-de-camp to the Prince. He was given a captain's commission, raised his own company and fought during the uprising with the Duke of Perth's regiment. After Culloden and his subsequent escape to Holland he eventually travelled to Paris, joined the French and served with them, and with Montcalm, in Canada.

His memoirs were first published in 1820 and in *The Forty-Five* (Folio Society, London, 1958) he wrote as follows of the build up to the fight at Clifton and of the battle / skirmish itself: 'On the 16th (December) our army passed the night at Shap, but our artillery remained at the distance of a league and a half from Kendal, some ammunition waggons having broken down, so that we were obliged to pass the whole night on the high road, exposed to a dreadful storm of wind and rain. On the 17th, the Prince, with the army, arrived at Penrith; but the artillery, with Lord George, and the regiments of the Macdonalds of Glengarry, consisting of five hundred men who remained with us to strengthen our ordinary escort, could only reach Shap, and that at great difficulty, at nightfall.

'We set out from Shap by break of day on the 18th to join the army, which waited for us at Penrith; but we had scarcely begun our march when we saw a great number of the enemy's light-horse continually hovering about us, without venturing, however, to come within musket shot. The appearance of these light-horse appeared the most extraordinary as, hitherto, we had seen none in the whole course of our expedition into England. We arrived at mid-day at the foot of an eminence about half way between Penrith and Shap, which it was necessary to cross in our march. The moment we began to ascend, we instantly discovered cavalry, marching two and two abreast on the top of the hill, who disappeared soon after as if to form themselves in order of battle with the intention of disrupting the passage (of the Jacobites back north). We heard, at the same time, a prodigious number of trumpets and kettle-drums. Mr Brown, colonel in the train of Lally's regiment, was at the head of the column, with two of the companies which the Duke of Perth had attached to the artillery, of which mine was one. After them followed the guns and ammunition waggons, and then the two other companies attached to the artillery. Lord George was in the rear of the column with the regiment of the Macdonalds.

'We stopped a moment at the foot of the hill, everybody believing it was the English army from the great number of trumpets and kettle-drums. In this seemingly desperate conjuncture, we immediately adopted the opinion of Mr Brown, and resolved to rush upon the enemy, sword in hand and open a passage to our army at Penrith, or perish in the attempt. Thus, without informing Lord George of our resolution, we darted forward with great swiftness, running up the hill as fast as our legs could carry us. Lord George, who was in the rear, seeing our manoeuvre at the head of the column, and being unable to pass the waggons in the deep roads confined by hedges in which we then were, immediately ordered the Highlanders to proceed across the enclosure, and ascend the hill from another quarter. They ran so fast that they reached the summit of the hill almost as soon as those who were at the head of the column. We were agreeably surprised when we reached the top to find, instead of the English army, only three hundred light-horse and chasseurs, who immediately fled in disorder. We were only able to come up with one man who had been thrown from his horse and whom we wished to make prisoner to obtain some intelligence from him. But it was impossible to save him from the fury of the Highlanders, who cut him to pieces in an instant. From the great number of trumpets and kettle-drums which the light-horse had with them, there is every reason for supposing that it was their design to endeavour to induce us to turn aside from the road to Penrith, by making us believe that the whole English army was on the hill before us. Had we fallen into the snare which was laid for us, in a few hours every man of our detachment would either have been killed or taken prisoner.

'We immediately resumed our march, but in less than an hour one of our ammunition waggons broke down from the badness of the roads and we were obliged to halt. The singular advantage of the light-horse had filled me with some uneasiness, as I was unable to account for their audacity. I communicated my fears to Mr Grant and, in order that we might not lose time in repairing the broken waggon, I suggested to him that we should go to a farm, which we saw on our right, and try to procure one. He consented and we took about seven or eight men with us, of whom my sergeant, Dickson, was one. Having found a waggon in the courtyard of the farmer, we immediately carried it off, and our march was retarded no longer than the time necessary for transferring the ammunition from one waggon to another. In returning from the farm, Dickson called our attention to something which appeared blackish to us, on a hill about four miles to our left. He alone, contrary to the opinion of everyone else, maintained that he saw it moving, and that it was the English army advancing towards us. As we took what he saw for bushes, and as nobody excepting himself could distinguish anything, I treated him as a visionary. But he still persisted, till I ordered him to be silent, telling him that fear alone could have filled his imagination with the idea of an army. However his last word was that we should see in an hour whether or not he was in the right.

'When we had advanced about two miles, we were soon convinced that Dickson's eyes were much better than ours. The Duke of Cumberland, having followed us by forced marches with two thousand cavalry and as many foot-soldiers mounted

behind them, fell suddenly on the Macdonalds, who were in the rear of the column, with all the fury and impetuosity imaginable. Fortunately the road running between thorn hedges and ditches, the cavalry could not act in such a manner to surround us, nor present a larger front to us than the breadth of the road. The Highlanders received their charge with the most undaunted firmness. They repelled the assailants with their swords, and did not quit their ground till the artillery and waggons were a hundred paces from them and continuing their rout (route). Then the Highlanders wheeled to the right and ran with full speed till they joined the waggons, when they stopped again for the cavalry, and stood their charge as firm as a wall. The cavalry were repulsed in the same manner as before by their swords. We marched in this manner about a mile, the cavalry continually renewing the charge and the Highlanders always repulsing them, repeating the same manoeuvre and behaving like lions.

'The Prince, at Penrith, having received an imperfect account of our adventure with the light-horse, immediately ordered the army to advance to our assistance. The English cavalry accompanied us in this manner till we arrived opposite the castle of Clifton-hall, which is three miles from Penrith. But halted as soon as they saw our army drawn up in order of battle. They then entered the enclosures of the castle, which were defended by thorn hedges, and, having dismounted, formed themselves in battle order in front of our army, which was upon a heath. The hedges separated the two armies, which were within a musket-shot of each other . . .

'The sun was setting when our detachments formed a junction (fought) with the

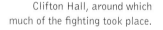
Clifton Hall, around which much of the fighting took place.

army. The Highlanders immediately ran to the enclosures where the English were, fell down on their knees, and began to cut down the thorn-hedges with their dirks; a necessary precaution as they wore no breeches, but only a sort of petticoat which reached to their knees. During this operation, they received the fire of the English with the most admirable firmness and constancy. As soon as the hedge was cut down, they jumped into the enclosures sword in hand, and, with an inconceivable intrepidity, broke the English battalions, who suffered so much the more as they did not turn their backs but allowed themselves to be cut to pieces without quitting their ground. Platoons of forty and fifty men might be seen falling all at once under the swords of the Highlanders; yet they still remained firm and closed up their ranks as an opening was made through them by the sword.

'At length, however, the Highlanders forced them to give way, and pursued them across three enclosures, to a heath which lay behind them. The only prisoner they took was the Duke of Cumberland's footman, who declared that his master would have been killed if the pistol, with which a Highlander took aim at his head, had not missed fire. The Prince had the politeness to send him back instantly to his master. We could not ascertain the loss of the English in this affair, which some estimated as high as six hundred men. We only lost a dozen Highlanders who, after traversing the enclosures, continued their pursuit with too much ardour along the heath.

'Our army did not withdraw from Clifton-hall til some hours after the night had set in but our artillery was sent off in the beginning of the action, with orders to continue to advance to Carlisle without stopping at Penrith. We learned, from the footman, that the Duke of Cumberland, having given all his trumpeters and kettle-drummers to the light-horse, had hoped to retard the march of our detachment with the artillery. If we had been in any manner the dupes of this artifice, we should all have been destroyed, for, in half an hour, the Duke would have got between us and our army, and our communication would thus have been cut off.

'As we very much dreaded the junction of Marshal Wade with these four thousand men, whom the Duke of Cumberland had brought with him to Clifton-hall by forced marches, to harass us in our retreat, as well as the arrival of the rest of his army which he had left behind him, we marched all night and arrived at Carlisle about

There is a story that a skeleton of one of the Jacobites, clad in tartan, was found years after the battle in the hollowed out centre of an oak.

seven o'clock in the morning of 19th of December. Next morning, before the break of day, we quitted Carlisle . . .'

The Chevalier de Johnstone continued: ' . . . We left Carlisle on the 20th of December at three o'clock in the morning (Carlisle Castle and its occupying force of Jacobites was left to the mercy of the English – it was retaken on December 30th after a siege involving canon brought from Whitehaven) and arrived on the banks of the River Esk, which separates Scotland from England, about two in the afternoon. This river, which is usually shallow, had been swelled by an incessant rain of several days to a depth of four feet. We were obliged to cross it immediately, lest a continuation of the rain during the night should render the passage altogether impracticable. Our position had become extremely critical. We had not only to encounter all the English troops, but likewise the Hessians and Swiss, with six thousand Dutch, of the garrisons of Dendermonde and Tournai, who had been landed in England.

'Nothing could be better arranged than the passage of the river (the crossing was apparently made just south of Longtown). Our cavalry formed in the river, to break the force of the current, about twenty five paces above that part of the ford where our infantry were to pass: the Highlanders formed themselves into ranks of ten or twelve abreast, with their arms locked in such a manner as to support one another against the rapidity of the river, leaving sufficient intervals between their ranks for the passage of the water. Cavalry were likewise stationed in the river, below the ford, to pick up and save those who might be carried away by the violence of the current. The interval between the cavalry appeared like a paved street through the river, the heads of the Highlanders being generally all that was seen above the water. By means of this contrivance, our army passed the Esk in an hour's time, without losing a single man, and a few girls, determined to share the fortune of their lovers, were the only persons who were carried away by the rapidity of the stream. Fires were kindled to dry our people as soon as they quitted the water and the bagpipers having commenced playing, the Highlanders began all to dance, expressing the utmost joy on seeing their country again – forgetting the chagrin which had incessantly devoured them, and which they had continually nourished ever since their departure from Derby.'

Despite the sound of the pipes and the fleeting joy at being back on Scottish soil, it was all a far cry from the day, little over a month before, when Bonnie Prince Charlie rode victorious on a white charger into Carlisle.

As the conflict at Clifton unfolded fires were burning on the summits of Helvellyn and Skiddaw, warning of the relative closeness of the rebels. In a land without the light pollution we have today the fires glowed red and must have been visible for many miles. Local people, not surprisingly, were frightened of the rebels who were thought of as being unkempt, violent, unruly and wild. On the road south, with Bonnie Prince Charlie campaigning for support, their behaviour may have been tempered by the cause, although this was not always the case. In his book *Bonnie Prince Charlie in Cumberland* (published 1903) J.A. Wheatley wrote:  'About noon several hundreds, described as wretched, ill-looking, shabby crew, armed with targets, broadswords and muskets, arrived at Naworth Castle and seemed very angry that no deference was paid to their flag. That afternoon and the next day they spent in shooting sheep and geese and robbing on the highway. Their chiefs expressed great dissatisfaction but could not restrain them.' The riff-raff of the Jacobite army were described by one writer as Shabroons and by Dr Waugh, Chancellor of Carlisle, as Walie-draigles, a title which suggests it wasn't intended as a compliment.

On the return journey the less reputable Jacobites were probably increasingly desperate and lawless, especially when some of the local populace attempted to pick them off as they retreated. On a day-to-day basis the officers and the gentlemen could invariably find semi-decent accommodation but the soldiers in the field undoubtedly had a tough time. Hardened as they were it must still have been a pretty miserable existence, especially in the depths of winter, marching all night on occasion, wading ice-cold rivers and sleeping rough in sodden fields and woods or, at best, outhouses. Food would be scarce and what wasn't provided by the army the rebels would steal. Homes were pillaged. There were even scare stories that the wildest, ugliest and hungriest of the rebels ate babies.

But what ever the rebel low life got up to the Government forces under The Duke of Cumberland and his cohorts more than made up for post Culloden as they turned the Highlands into a bloodbath under the guise of ensuring that of uprisings there were nae mair.

Among others who made observations on the clash at Clifton was a resident of the village, a Quaker by the name of Thomas Savage, who farmed with his son, Jonathan, at Clifton End Farm. In correspondence to a friend, Richard Partridge, dated December 29th, 1745 (a day before Carlisle Castle was retaken by The Duke of Cumberland), he wrote: 'As to the rebels, when they came south we did not suffer much, but they seemed to have great confidence that they would proclaim their King in London, on the 24th of last month, and crown him on New Year's day, and then they would send Geordy (King George II, the reigning monarch of the time) over to Hanover, and would tread down his turnip-field dykes; highly dises-teeming the Duke (the Duke of Cumberland was King George II's son) calling him Geordy's Lad and Geordy's Wully, with many more approbrious speeches; but on their return north they were cruelly barbarous and inhuman when here, for their leaders gave them liberty to plunder for four hours and then to burn Lowther, Clifton and Penrith, and some say for six miles around . . . they had sent off a party of their horse to plunder and burn Lowther Hall and town, and were also plundering our town, leaving nothing they could lay their hands on, breaking locks and making ruinous work, even to all our victuals and little childrens' clothes of all sorts.'

In the action that ensued at Clifton, Thomas Savage and his son went out of their way to warn the Government forces of the danger they faced, through ambush, in the village. So much so that the son, Jonathan – who had ventured out to try and bring cattle to safety – was intercepted by the Jacobites: 'Four rebels on horseback seized him, calling him a spy, and had him down under their horses' feet, swearing desperately many times they would shoot him; three of them commanded the fourth to shoot him, which he attempted with his gun, and then pistol, but neither would fire, so he escaped and came in (to the farm house) a little after.'

Thomas Savage continued: 'Now, it beginning to grow dark, the rebels were so thick about the house we had no hope of saving ourselves, but we concluded on leaving the house and go into the fields, if we could but get there. In the middle of the orchard we were parted by the rebels, one part of us driven into the fields, and the other part into the house, severely threatening our lives, never expecting to see one another alive again. A son-in-law and his family were under like circumstances, for they seemed more severe upon us than upon others. We were not all got to the fire side before the firing, on all hands, was dreadful, which continued half an hour, in which time were killed 10 of the King's men and 21 wounded, and the Duke's footman taken prisoner, and of the rebels five killed and many wounded.

'By early morning were 30 prisoners under custody, and after the heat of firing was over all seemed still a little space, after which some came and broke in at my court door, calling sharply to open; but we believed it to be the rebels and would not open, when they begun to be sharp and orders were given to fire, they supposing the house to be full of rebels; but I called and said I would open as fast as I could and the first words said to me were: "Could the Duke lodge here tonight?" To which, with pleasure, I answered "yes", and pleasant, agreeable company he was – a man of parts, very friendly, and no pride in him. Much on his head I could say, if it would not be tedious to thee, and yet I shall mention one thing more to thee, very remarkable, which was, our cattle were all standing amongst the slain men and not one of them hurt and them that were banished from our house came in again next morning, which the Duke's men said was a wonder they were not all killed, our next neighbour being shot at the same time . . .'

The pacifist Quaker clearly saw the Government forces as being their salvation: 'Thanks to the Most High, whose power is above the power of man, often preventing wicked designs, it was certainly the Lord's doing in bringing forward the noble Duke

The stone in the graveyard of St Cuthbert's Church, Clifton, marking the grave of the Government soldiers who died in battle.

and his men in the very hour of great distress; as for my own part, I must ever love and esteem him as a man of worth.'

Thomas Savage might not have had such a high opinion of The Duke of Cumberland in the light of what happened after Culloden, the summary justice and, subsequent to that, the barbaric retribution visited on rebels who were captured and eventually brought to trial.

The Duke of Cumberland, in his account of the skirmish, wrote: 'What the rebels may have lost I can't tell; we have four officers wounded, none mortally, and about 40 men killed and wounded. The regiment which suffered the greatest loss was the King's Own Regiment of Dragoons. By some confusion in the two dismounted squadrons commanded by Colonel Honeywood, they firing at 150 yards distance, and then giving way, the rebels came out with broadswords and wounded several of the officers, and some of the men. When the officers of the King's regiment were wounded, the rebels cried "No quarter, murder them" and they received several wounds after they were knocked down.'

The Colonel Honeywood referred to had fought at the Battle of Dettingen (Bavaria) in 1743 and had there suffered 23 broadsword cuts and was shot twice, the two musket balls having never been extracted. At Clifton Moor he was in the wars again. One of the Highland prisoners who was asked about the fight recalled: "We got on vary weel, till the lang man in the muckel boots came ower the dyke, but his foot slipped on a turd (probably a cow pat) and we gat him down." This, indeed, was the somewhat unfortunate Colonel Honeywood who on this occasion received three sword cuts to the head and was taken to nearby Howgill Castle – which he owned – to recover from his latest wounds. He also lost his sword at Clifton, this being claimed by Cluny, Chief of the Macphersons, as a trophy of war.

Clifton today is a typical working Cumbrian village, situated close to the main West Coast rail line and the M6 motorway – fast routes to London in comparison to the ponderous trail of an 18th Century army travelling on foot and horseback. Several of its current old buildings and farmsteads were in place at the time of the battle of Clifton Moor. These include St Cuthbert's Church, 800 years old, where the Government soldiers are buried, a recent (2005) gravestone in the churchyard, near the gate, reads: 'In memory of the troopers of Blands Regiment who lie here. Killed on Clifton Moor 1745. Presented by The Queen's Royal Hussars 2005.' Records suggest that 10 are buried there.

Nearby is Clifton Hall. The church and the hall are positioned virtually opposite each other on an S bend on the Penrith side to the north of the village. The heaviest fighting took place in the environs and enclosures of Clifton Hall, a 14th Century manor house, once much bigger and widespread than the distinctive pele tower and its rooms, all that now remains of the original building, but nonetheless still very impressive.

At the southern end of the village are Town End Farm and the adjacent Town End Cottage, home of the Quaker Thomas Savage and where the Duke of Cumberland stayed the night after the battle. Across the road are the George and Dragon and, down a lonning, The Rebel Tree where the Jacobites are buried. On display boards at the George and Dragon there was at one time an exhibition of artwork by children from Clifton School depicting scenes from the battle. The images were colourful and in their simplicity provided an unintentionally sanitised view of the brutal reality of the 18th Century warfare that took place in the village almost 300 years ago and for which the Rebel Tree is now a stark but not solitary reminder.

\* Soil nan Gaidheal. The Scottish organisation dedicated to the concept of a free and independent Scotland, focussing on history, heritage and culture.

\*Crann Tara. 'Aims and objectives include preserving and maintaining the history, culture and heritage of Scotland, passing on the knowledge in the hope that it will keep the country in safe hands. The group was formed in the wake of the 700th anniversary of William Wallace's murder in London, 23rd of August 2005.'

St Cuthbert's Church, Clifton.

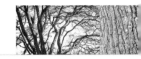

# THE CAPON TREE
## Hung, drawn and quartered

*7*

It is a place of light and dark, all of which will soon become apparent.

On the fringes of Brampton, on the line of the old paved road from Newcastle to Carlisle, is a tall, slender stone monument called the Capon Tree Memorial. The tree itself was an oak and received its name, Capon, for a variety of reasons, some of which are depicted in carvings in an unusual wooden bench situated at the side of the lane and near to the original site of the tree, a small clearing situated in a half circle of mature beech trees. The Capon Tree once stood in the centre on the exact spot where the stone monument now holds pride of place. The tree is no more; it finally crumbled many years ago, most probably at some point in the mid 19th Century.

The Capon Tree Memorial at Brampton.

The carving on a seat nearby depicting the tree and some of its uses.

The distinctive carvings on the gently curved back rest of the bench show a tree with outspread branches and beneath the foliage are what appears (from left to right) to be two men looking on; a man celebrating; a boxing match; a noose hanging from a bough; a man sitting upright against the trunk of the tree and eating a meal; a courting couple in an embrace; two children playing a ball game; swallows in flight and a woman, with a dog at her feet, waving farewell to a traveller who has a stick over his shoulders, á la Dick Whittington, with a small bundle at the end that presumably contains all his worldly possessions. Each carving has some significance that relates to the tree and its history.

The monument where the tree once stood commemorates one really dark episode of this particular corner of Cumbria, a story that is represented by the noose in the carvings on the bench.

For the moment let's focus on the light and enter into the speculation on how the Capon Tree got its name. The tree, situated at an important point on the old Roman road, was a meeting place for judges as they made their way to and from Newcastle

The remains of the Capon Tree as drawn by the Rev W. Ford in 1833. Image from the Transactions of the Cumberland and Westmorland Antiquarian and Archaelogical Society.

to Carlisle for the assizes. A popular theory has it that they enjoyed lunch under the boughs of the tree and that one of their favourite dishes was capon, otherwise known as chicken or, to be more precise, a domestic cock castrated and fattened for eating; washed down with wine.

Perhaps that is how the Capon Tree got its name? Could it be that simple? The plot, however, soon thickens and I am indebted to the thorough detective work of the Cumberland and Westmorland Antiquarian and Archaelogical Society and the findings of their very own Hercule Poirot, one Henry Penfold (note they share the same initials), who in the society's transactions for 1904, delivered at a meeting of the society in Carlisle on April 19th of that year (and later contained in the society's literature) poured a little scorn, not to mention cold water, on the more widely held theory relating to cockerels, castrated or otherwise.

'The consideration of three maps, all of recent date, have led to the writing of this paper,' Henry told his assembled audience. 'On the first, of date 1777, we find marked "The Capon Tree"; on the second, the earliest Ordnance Survey, we find marked "The Remains of the Capon Tree"; while on the most recent map the spot is marked "Site of the Capon Tree." This progressive marking of the name justified the placing on record all that is known of this once famous tree; all the more was this necessary when practically nothing in the way of documentary evidence has come down to us to show its original significance and meaning.

'The Capon Tree in the minds of the inhabitants of this north-eastern corner of the county was associated with many venerable traditions and stories, and we may find it a necessary though an unpleasant task to unshroud this venerable oak and to clear away the fairy tales — of judges under its branches regaling themselves on capons and wine, of the popularly supposed idea that this tree was the place where thousands of border raiders were executed, of tales of Capon Tree boggles; these and many others just as mythical will have to disappear under the plain light of history.'

Returning to the question of the capon-guzzling judges, Henry Penfold refers to the words of Lord Macauley provided in no less a volume than the *History of England*, Volume 1, Chapter 3: 'No traveller ventured into that country (Cumberland and Westmorland) without making his will. The Judges on Circuit with the whole body of barristers, attorneys, clerks and serving men rode on horseback from Newcastle to Carlisle, armed, and escorted by a strong guard under the command of the Sheriffs. It was necessary to carry provisions, for the country was a wilderness which afforded no supplies. The spot where the cavalcade halted to dine, under an immense oak, is not yet forgotten.'

Henry Penfold goes on to add his own observations: 'This reference to the Capon Tree is grounded on *Hutchinson's History* (Hutchinson's History of Cumberland, published 1794) and though as we have already seen there is reason to discredit the story of the Judges dining on capons and other comestibles, there is no room to doubt that they rested under this tree, which stood on such a convenient place for that purpose. The old road by which it stood is a continuation of the ancient Stanegate or Carelgate (old Roman road), the Northumberland portion of which can still be partly traced. We believe also that a considerable portion of it in Cumberland in the Brampton locality can also be traced. Another reason for believing that the cavalcade halted here is that the tree was a very large one, and though when Hutchinson wrote it was then in great decay, from the picture drawn by Rev. W. Ford in 1833 we can in some measure imagine what it had been in its prime. The disappearance of the tree has been hastened by the zeal of the younger portion of the population, who used to knock pieces off and take them away as curiosities. Every vestige of this once majestic oak has now gone, but we are glad to know that the site has been (August, 1904) permanently marked by a graceful and appropriate memorial.'

Warming to his meticulous task, Henry continues: 'The tree gives the name to a small farm of thirty or forty acres which, in 1778, the year of the making of the Brampton award (under the Enclosure Act), was sold for the purpose of the payment of the expenses and ever since has borne the name of Capon Tree Farm. By the kindness of Lord Carlisle we have examined his valuable collection of estate maps in the muniment room at Naworth, but as the tree stood on common land – land from time immemorial common to the parishioners and therefore not on the Naworth estate – the more ancient of these maps do not contain evidence even of the existence of the tree. From a rare map of the county of Cumberland previous to the passing of the Enclosure Act, and belonging to Mr. Alderman Dobson, we find the tree marked at the very extreme corner of the common land, the property of Lord Carlisle. From this map of date 1777, as well as from the plan accompanying the award and dated 1778, we see this tree marked alone with no other trees near it. Indeed it is the only tree on the plan issued with the award, a plan which covered 1,760 acres of common land which lay in Brampton parish. This alone is some indication of the importance attached to it both by the parishioners and the makers of the award. Was not this then a likely place for a Bramptonian to gratify one of the only pieces of pure sentiment that a Cumbrian indulges, namely, of setting his friends out on the road or meeting them there when going or returning on their way? Perhaps this has some bearing on the name Capon Tree . . .

'Before proceeding we might in passing note that there are another two Capon Trees known to us - one in the pasture at Alnwick Castle, and the other a solitary remaining member of Jed Forest standing near Ferniehurst Castle, Jedburgh, on the estate of the Marquis of Lothian. How then did these trees, all ancient oaks, get the name?'

George Tate's *History of Alnwick* revealed that a favourite pastime of girls was played under the branches of the Capon Tree and was accompanied by a peculiar local song. The name indicates the character of the game. Kep is from the Anglo-Saxon Cepan, Teutonic Kappan, to catch or capture, for when the game was played the ball was thrown into the air and kepped, or intercepted in its descent by one or other of the girls and it was then thrown up again to be caught or intercepted by some other, singing at the same time the following ditty:

*Keppy ball, Keppy ball, coban tree.*
*Come down the long lonning and tell to me*
*The form and the features, the speech and degree,*
*Of the man that is my true love to be.*
*One a maiden, two a wife.*
*Three a maiden, four a wife . . .*

And so on. The numbers were continued so long as the ball could be kept rebounding against the tree. Capon, coban and covin, were several names of the same tree, the letters p, b and v being interchangeable. Other possible explanations for the meaning of the name relate to the tree being a meeting place. In respect of the tree at Jedburgh this could signify the place where the clans met in olden time, hence the name of Capon from the Scotch word 'kep' – to meet.

But Henry Penfold would not let those old assize judges off lightly.

'Nor can we leave this part of our subject without alluding to Hutchinson's idea of the derivation of the name,' he continues apace. 'He tells us that the name is derived from Judges regaling themselves under its branches with a repast, the principal courses of which were capons and wine; a story repeated also by Lord Macaulay in his *History of England*. This appears to be the most fanciful attempt to give the origin of the name, for while it might be a fact that the Judges en route from Newcastle to Carlisle regaled themselves as stated, this could not by any possible manner of means be the explanation of the name when applied to the two trees at Alnwick and Ferniehurst. We are therefore compelled to seek elsewhere for the meaning.'

Henry, having dismissed the hungry judges theory out of hand, directs us to the Anglo Saxon and the meaning of the word in *Bosworth's Dictionary* where Cepan is 'to take, hold, go about, endeavour, make an attempt, betake oneself to, seek after, catch at, heed, regard, catch, keep.'

'We do not strain the meaning then when we put down the Capon Tree at Brampton as the trysting tree,' explains Henry, ever the romantic, 'the meeting place of the

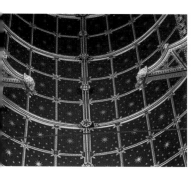

The spectacular ceiling of Carlisle Cathedral.

Carlisle Cathedral in all its splendour with its ceiling and the magnificent stained glass of the East Window. Amazing to think that part of the building provided a squalid prison for Jacobites after Carlisle Castle was retaken by The Duke of Cumberland.

district, to which lovers betook themselves, where friends met friends and where they accompanied them to on their outward journey and sped the parting guest.'

And there's more . . . 'Mr. Wm. Barker of the Sands, Brampton, an old residenter informs us that the Capon Tree was the rendezvous where all those who in Brampton were inclined for fisticuffs met their opponents. He says that on fair, market, or hiring days, the man who considered himself cock of the neighbourhood shook the bull ring in the market place, as a sign that he was ready to meet any one who disputed his championship. The opponents always repaired to the Capon Tree and in the presence of such backers as assembled, fought for the supremacy. There is no evidence whatever of the rhyming game of Keppy ball having been played against the trunk of the ancient oak, though even if it were so, it is likely that with the tree having become a gallows, the innocent play of the children would be stopped or removed to some less gruesome landmark.'

Henry Penfold has clearly reached the conclusion that the most likely explanation for the name Capon Tree is that it was an old established meeting place, a rendezvous where travellers were welcomed or were wished a fond farewell on their journeys; the trysting tree where lovers would meet and also where the hard men of the area met to fight for supremacy with wagers on the outcome of the bare-knuckle boxing bouts. Draw your own conclusions.

Regrettably, the Capon Tree is also associated with another event and it is here that we go from the light to the dark in this story of a tree. The little market town of Brampton played a significant role in the Jacobite uprisings of 1715 and 1745. The Jacobite army marched into Brampton in November 1715 proclaiming The Pretender and introducing an excise on malt and ale with which to pay the Highlanders sixpence per head per day to keep them in good order and under command. Thirty years on in November 1745 Prince Charles Edward Stuart 'passed over this old road, and entered Brampton by the Lonning,' Henry Penfold informed the antiquarian society. 'Two or three days later the Mayor and Corporation passed the tree when going and returning on their errand of delivering upon bended knees the keys of the city to their conqueror at Brampton. Prince Charles himself, also, on Monday, the 18th

Carlisle Castle.    November, 1745, left Brampton on his white charger, preceded by his hundred pipers in full Highland panoply, and took possession of the city – the proudest act and the proudest day of his romantic career . . .' His headquarters in Brampton were situated at The Joiners Arms in High Cross Street and a French sword and bonnet (now at the Tullie House Museum in Carlisle) were found in the town's Half Moon Inn, and were purported to be owned by the French ambassador representing France on Charles's behalf. The prince's triumphant ride into Carlisle was arguably the highpoint of his campaign. The prince was proclaimed King of England at the cross in the market place in the heart of Carlisle.

'Nine months later,' reported Henry Penfold, 'a procession of six Jacobite sufferers were drawn on hurdles up the old highway, the place of execution being the Capon Tree.'

The horrendous retribution that followed the final defeat of the Jacobites at Culloden was not restricted to Scotland. Apart from the brutality of the pacification across the

Highlands, many prisoners were hauled off for trial and execution elsewhere. Of 3,471 prisoners documented, 120 were executed; 936 were transported; 222 were banished; 88 died in prison; 58 escaped from prison; 76 received a conditional pardon; 1,287 were released or exchanged and the disposal of 684 was unknown. In Cumberland six Jacobites were executed by hanging from the Capon Tree at Brampton on October 21, 1746; twenty had previously suffered a similar fate at Carlisle on Harraby Hill and six at Penrith, the place of execution being raised ground between the White Ox and Airgill Castle.

In Carlisle, 396 prisoners were taken when the castle surrendered to The Duke of Cumberland. They were held in terrible conditions in the cathedral and in the castle. Many were sent elsewhere in January 1746, to Lancaster and Chester, to be held until they were put on trial.

Of the prisoners in the cathedral it was noted afterwards: 'The rebels made a most nasty church which will not be fit for service for a long while; and left the smallpox of which many of our soldiers (there was a strong military presence in the form of guards) have fallen down and some dead. The flags being old, spungy and ill-laid the earth under them corrupted and till that is removed the cathedral church will not be safe to have service in it.'

It was, in fact, not until the end of February 1746, after 'much burning of sulphur and tar' that the cathedral was used once again as a place of worship as opposed to a temporary prison. Visiting the cathedral today it is difficult to imagine that the building was once used in such a way. It is a magnificent building with the fantastic stained glass of the celebrated East window, the glory of its star-filled, gold on blue ceiling (designed by the architect Owen Jones and based on his studies of Islamic decoration in the Alhambra Palace, Granada) and a wonderful sense of calm. While I am not an overtly religious person I regularly visit the cathedral and find that time spent there in the peace and quiet of its walls, away from the rush and roar of the traffic, vehicular and otherwise, is good for the soul.

When the Assizes was held in Carlisle in August 1746, 382 prisoners, from all quarters (Lancaster, Newcastle, Whitehaven and Scotland) were assembled. It became clear that there were too many to be put on trial so the prisoners drew lots. Eventually 127 stood trial at Carlisle, the 'lucky' ones were transported for life. All of the prisoners were held in the most appalling conditions.

The Brampton six were among the many incarcerated in the small dungeon in the keep of Carlisle Castle where the only light and ventilation was supplied by a narrow slit. The deprivation was such that the prisoners licked a small part of the wall where meagre amounts of water trickled down. The eroded areas of local red sandstone, the licking stones, where the prisoners attempted to moisten their parched mouths and throats, can still be seen. Prisoners elsewhere were also kept in abysmal conditions with only offal for food, many on ships in the Thames after sea journeys from Scotland; others died long before they got to trial. The six who were executed at Brampton were confined at Carlisle Castle from August 12th, 1746 until their date of execution on October 21st.

Inscribed on the tall stone monument that is the Capon tree memorial is the following: 'This stone is placed to mark the site of the ancient capon tree under whose shade The Judges of Assize rested and upon whose branches were executed October XXI MDCCXLVI for adherence to the cause of the Royal line of Stewart

Colonel James Innes
Captain Patrick Lindesay
Ronald Macdonald
Thomas Parr
Peter Taylor
Michael Dellard

Beneath the memorial, when I visited, was a bouquet of white carnations and a note in memory of the six. The words on it were smudged by the weather and could not be read, other than the words 'alba gu brath' (Scotland forever).

The executions were not simply hangings. These were brutal times and the penalty for high treason was to be hung, drawn and quartered. The unfortunate victims were pinioned and carried to the place of execution on a wooden hurdle covered with straw and drawn by a horse. At the gallows they were hung by the neck for three minutes

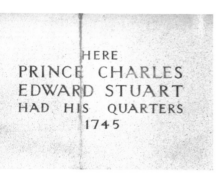

Words engraved in the stone above the entrance to Marks and Spencer, Carlisle, once the Earl's Inn where Bonnie Prince Charlie and The Duke of Cumberland had their quarters in 1745 and 1746, respectively.

or longer and then cut down, stripped naked and, some still alive or showing signs of life, their bowels and heart were cut out and flung onto a fire. In some instances the victims were also castrated before being disembowelled. The head was severed and the body cut into four. Parts of the body, but especially the head, were preserved in spirits and distributed to different parts of the country and placed on spikes at significant points such as city gates; a warning to others and a grisly reminder of what happened if you opposed king and country.

HERE
THE DUKE OF
CUMBERLAND
HAD HIS QUARTERS
1746

In Carlisle the heads of Thomas Chadwick and John Berwick, both executed at Kennington Common, London, on July 30th, 1746, for high treason, were displayed on English Gate. Chadwick and Berwick were among those captured when Carlisle Castle surrendered and they would, on being sent to London for trial and subsequent execution, have passed beneath the very gates on which their severed heads would later be displayed. For several years after the executions heads adorned the various city gates and it is recorded that the two on English Gate were still in position in 1766. To fix them an iron spike was driven through the head. The spike had a small circular plate on which the head rested. A similar plate was riveted to the top of the skull and the spike was soldered into the stone of the gate. It was built to last.

The executioner in Cumberland was William Stout, of Hexham, who was appointed for a sum of twenty guineas. As a bonus he also got the clothes of the victims. Stout was apparently bad to the bone and gave every sign of enjoying his notoriety and the slaughter.

Of those who died at Brampton three were Highlanders, two Englishmen and one Irishman; three were Roman Catholics and three Protestants. Four other prisoners were to have been executed along with the six but James Forbes, Richard Morison, and Alexander Hutchinson were reprieved while the fourth, Stephen Fitzgerald, died in prison. Those who were reprieved, or among those who had been fortunate when lots were drawn to see who would stand trial and who would not, were transported to the Colonies. Severely weakened by the prison regime, few survived the experience.

It is not known what became of the bodies of those who were executed, but the remains of some of those killed in Carlisle, at Harraby Hill, were buried in St

Cuthbert's Churchyard in the centre of the city, a stone's throw from where Bonnie Prince Charlie had his headquarters, a fact that is marked to this day in words cut into the stone above the entrance to Marks and Spencer (formerly the Earl's Inn, owned by Mr Charles Highmore, Attorney at law): 'Here Prince Charles Edward Stuart had his quarters 1745.' In the store window display immediately below the words in the spring of 2010 (at the time I made a note) was a bikini-clad mannequin. On the other side of the doors at the same height and on the same stone panel is a similar message dated a year later and with a different name: 'Here The Duke of Cumberland had his quarters 1746.' Below these words the store window was promoting the latest brand in school uniforms.

Only a year separates the dates that the two stayed at the same HQ in the city as recorded in the words inscribed in stone above the entrance to a modern day store. But even in 21st Century Carlisle, it seems, the Duke of Cumberland continues to pursue Bonnie Prince Charlie down the centuries, forever and a day, world without end. Strangely enough the Prince and the Duke purportedly slept on the very same bed at Earl's Inn, admittedly a year apart. Presumably the bedding was changed in the interim.

The last word in this sorry story goes to Henry Penfold who, in an extract from an account of the time, recorded: 'We were told in our youth by an old lady, who, when a girl, was present at the execution of some of the rebels at Carlisle, that most of them (all fine young men) were not half dead when cut down; one of them actually struggled with the wretch who opened his bosom to pluck out his heart. The scene she said haunted her fancy for half a century, and she never reflected on it without a shudder.'

'It is possible,' Henry concluded, 'that many Bramptonians gazed on the same gruesome spectacle at the Capon Tree. Little wonder, indeed, is it then that the

Capon Tree got the reputation of being the resort of ghosts and boggles, and for at least a century after the execution loomed largely in the talk of the country folk. Why the Capon Tree was chosen or why the prisoners were brought to Brampton for execution cannot now accurately be discovered. Conjecture and surmise lead us to think that where the Prince had stayed the rebels were hung as a warning to those inhabitants who had been fascinated by the urbanity of his bearing and the romance of his undertaking — no less an undertaking than regaining a lost crown and kingdom.'

Bonnie Prince Charlie, of course, made good his escape to France. He died of natural causes in Rome on January 31st, 1788. Others were not so fortunate.

Among them were those who met William Stout the executioner for the first and last time at Brampton's Capon Tree and who were sent on their way to another world in a manner that no one, but no one, would ever have chosen.

The Citadel now stands in Carlisle on the original site of the English Gate to the city where the severed heads of Jacobites were displayed on spikes.

*Overleaf: Carlisle Castle.*

## IMGES 8
### Val Corbett's tree photographs

As this book unfolded it some became apparent that Val Corbett had far exceeded the expectation of providing images for the main chapters on specific trees, their immediate environment and the stories linked to the trees I had identified as core subjects. And so we decided that a chapter should be devoted entirely to Val's photographic work on the theme of trees, naturally, and in which we would publish a strong selection of alternative and complementary images.

These in themselves provided a wide range of photographs, including my personal favourites – the dramatic image of a fallen rowan near Caldbeck against an ominous storm-laden sky; the autumnal shades of woodland at Brundholme (my local territory); the fantastic picture of a snow-covered road and trees under a blue sky near Skelton; the striking picture of a solitary tree set against a Croglin sunset; the awesome image of sunlight slanting across the ancient oaks at Keskadale (see initial pages of book) and last, but certainly not least, the powerful photograph on the facing page of a solitary tree at Lowther in a winter coat and appearing out of the ice-cold mist against a backcloth of sheer blue sky.

The sunset tree at Croglin and the winter tree at Lowther were also potential options for the cover of the book but in the final analysis it was decided to go for an initial concept, that of a cover which showed a vast array of images, highly colourful, slightly wacky and more representative of the many trees and related topics in Jack's Yak.

Looking through the images in this book and in the following chapter I am sure that everyone will have their personal favourites but on one thing I feel sure we can all agree: the quality of Val Corbett's photography is something else.

This spectacular image of a tree in its winter coat set against a sheer blue sky was taken in Lowther Park.

Overleaf: This fallen rowan is situated on the old road from Uldale to Caldbeck, just beyond the point where the road takes a sharp turn at Ellerbeck Common between dry stone walls to climb the hill towards Carlisle.

Graffiti on one of the Rusland
beeches in south Cumbria.

Beeches by the side of the road
near Bewcastle.

A solitary oak in winter.
This tree is situated on the
popular promontory by the side
of the water at Buttermere,
near Crag Wood.

Trees in their winter finery at Lowther Park.

Tough. A yew tree on Yewbarrow Scar.

A room with a view. A tree in a sheepfold near Nenthead.

Autumn colours at Glencoyne, Ullswater.

A woodland path by the water.
Autumn comes to Talkin Tarn.

Pine tree and wall at Silverdale.

Oak on a crag overlooking
Derwentwater with Blencathra's
distinctive form in the distance.

Flowering crab apple at
Yanwath.

Bluebell wood at Grizedale.

The ivy takes over from a faded
carving on a beech at Rusland.

An ash on the fellside near Tebay.

Autumn colours in Brundholme Wood on the slopes of Latrigg with Skiddaw in the background. The River Greta and the path following the old Keswick to Penrith railway line are in the cut between the two sets of trees in the image.

The ancient oaks at Keskadale.

Previous pages: An amazing winter scene on the road near Skelton where the pattern of the wispy cloud in a blue sky and the flow of the snow-covered road and wall, the gate, the shadows, the hedge and the tree-lined route all combine to create an exceptionally powerful image. Jaw dropping.

A solitary tree on the horizon at sunset.

A lush summer world of vegetation and trees by the roadside.

An avenue of beech provide the perfect carpet for carriages at Lowther Park.

Snow and ice in the branches
create a crazy formation.

A beech-bedecked path at
Loughrigg Terrace,
near Grasmere.

On closer inspection. Images
from woodland.

Previous pages: Tripping the light fantastic. Images of sunlight through the trees at Lowther.

A holly in summer and in winter over Haweswater.

Hedges have grown into full-blown trees in this picture of farmland near Appleby.

Let no man split asunder. A tree appears to have prised apart this rock at Easedale.

Woodland on a hillside near the River Brathay.

Images of winter . . . snow
and frost-laden trees by the
River Eamont. Silver birch and
sunlight in the Eden Valley and
trees on the shoreline at Calf
Close Bay, Derwentwater, with
the frozen, snow-covered lake
just beyond.

This image of a silver birch and the mist rising from the water at Ullswater makes me think of a spectacular firework.

The ancient oak at Keskadale.

A tree stands its ground at Lowther.

Hawthorn in bloom complements the white of the sheep in this image taken back o' Skiddaw.

Overleaf: Putting on a show. Frost and snow in the branches of trees on the shores of Ullswater.

# THE SPANISH CHESTNUT
## A legacy from Rome *9*

In the colourfully historic world of Muncaster Castle with its legions of rhododendrons, ranks of pungent skunk cabbages, and things that go bump in the night, there was once a man, a certain Thomas Skelton, or Tom Fool he (hence the phrase tomfoolery) who was jester to the Lord of Muncaster and his kin in the 16th or 17th Century and who wore a long multi-coloured coat, had something of a sinister cut to his jib and who once decapitated a luckless castle joiner who had the audacity to boast of his (the joiner's) love affair with the daughter of the household, one Heloise. Honour was at stake and Skelton – while not I suspect particularly honourable in word or deed – duly obliged his masters with a hammer and chisel. The severed head was hidden in wood shavings which it would doubtless stain blood red. There is something devilishly appropriate about a carpenter's head in his own shavings.

On other occasions, by way of entertainment – if these tales handed down over the centuries are to be believed – Thomas Skelton sat at the foot of a lovely Spanish chestnut beneath the castle walls, from which the views out to the sea and the Lakeland fells are fabulous, and, if he didn't like the look of you when you came along asking for directions, would send you to your death in the quick sands out on the bay. On one such occasion he pointed an unsuspecting traveller towards a 'safe' point for crossing and reassured his intended victim that a family of nine had safely negotiated the water there earlier in the day. What he failed to mention was that it was a family of geese.

As you may have gathered he was not a particularly nice piece of work and as you look into his eyes in the forbidding and very large portrait of Thomas Skelton that hangs at the end of a hallway atop a flight of stairs in the castle you will see exactly what I mean. The eyes follow you and they are, I think, mean and evil to the core. Or, at the very least, down right nasty and belonging to someone

The Spanish Chestnut above a daffodil-covered slope in front of Muncaster Castle.

Oil painting of Thomas Skelton in Muncaster Castle.

whom you should not trust to give you directions across the bay. And in the event of him walking off the wall armed with a hammer and chisel it would most definitely be the right time to make a quick exit. I suspect he was a psychopath.

Skip forward a few hundred years to the early years of the 21st Century and the end of its first eventful decade and the current occupant of Muncaster Castle, Patrick Gordon-Duff-Pennington is sitting against the trunk of the Spanish chestnut tree, doubtless in a similar position to that previously occupied by the aforementioned Thomas Skelton once upon a time. Patrick has kindly agreed to have his likeness taken by the photographer Val Corbett. This is a pleasure for him as he has already told me that Val is one of his most favourite people and he greeted her with a kiss and then another on her departure, removing his hat as he did so; ever the gentleman.

The bank below the tree is awash with daffodils, the rhododendron have yet to show their true colours and the skunk cabbages are just beginning to honk. The gnarled, old, and storm-thrashed Chestnut is situated a few knightly strides from the castle walls and commands a stunning view out over the Eskdale Valley to the Lakeland fells beyond. The landscape of Eskdale and the snaking River Esk roll out in all their splendour as you look out from the vantage point of the tree on its promontory. The valley is a lush green intersected only by a barely visible road, the A595, its line given away by vehicles rising above the hedge rows and dry stone walls to cross a neatly-arched 1828 road bridge built in stone over the Esk. The low land is enclosed by the valley with Muncaster Fell, Scafell, Bow Fell, Crinkle Crags, Hardknott, Eskdale Fell, Harter Fell, Birkby Fell and Ulpha Fell leading the eye round towards the coast and beyond to Black Combe, a whale-back of a mountain looking out to sea and one that invariably reminds me of the Millom poet Norman Nicholson.

*Beyond the wide*
*Sunset-glow cirrus of blast-furnace smoke,*
*My father saw it fly*
*Its thirty-seven-million-mile-long kite*
*Across Black Combe's black sky*
(extract from Nicholson's poem *Halley's Comet*)

Patrick himself is a poet and as Val takes his image under the tree we talk about trees and he recites lines, from memory, from one of his pieces in his anthology entitled *Patrick of the Hills*:

*We planted the trees today*
*In the sight of the sea,*
*And in the shadow of the seagulls' wings.*
*It was an act of grace,*
*Not so graceful as the arc of the white birds' flight,*
*But an act of faith and defiance*
*None the less,*
*One small atom of dust to fling*
*In the eyes of the world's destroyers*
*With their bombs*
*And their pledge to kill,*
*It will solve no problems*

*For a starving world.*
*Serve no material benefit*
*But to those who come after it will show*
*That we had a belief which sustained us.*

*And so today, we planted the trees*
*Underneath the wheeling wings,*
*With the breeze in our faces,*
*And in our minds*
*The thought of the shading leaves*
*Over the generation to come.*

Sadly the Spanish chestnut, not unlike Patrick, has seen better days. It is reputed to be 600 years old and limbs keep falling from it in storms.

"This tree is very much a part of our lives and we are terrified at what would happen if it fell down," says Patrick, who is 80 and tells me he suffered a heart attack six weeks before my visit and the medication is making him grumpy. "Our lives would be completely devastated. Last year in January it dropped a branch through our sitting room window which wasn't very kind of it. Luckily it didn't knock the house down. But it's old and it's beautiful and it stands in the landscape against Scafell and against Eskdale as a keeper of time and it's wonderful."

Drawing of Muncaster with anglers in the foreground and the castle on the hill.

The rich colours of Muncaster woodland with Eskdale beyond.

After fortifying himself (presumably against doctor's orders) with a lump of cake and a cup of coffee, Patrick took me on a tour of the gardens and the grounds. Val, bless her, is still taking it easy after breaking a leg on a ski-ing holiday. But Patrick has a spring in his step and is perhaps testing the water after his flirtation with St Peter. He was, he says, taken to hospital in Whitehaven after the heart attack and then, from there, to Middlesbrough. When he awoke in the whiteness of the hospital ward surrounded by angelic nurses he thought he was in heaven. But no, he was in Middlesbrough, a place that only infrequently is likened to heaven.

Patrick has a habit of confronting his mortality with a smile. He says he was "born a revolting child and has continued" and now that he is much older "deserves to be dead but hasn't quite made it." I find him likeable, informative and entertaining. He is one of those people who other people tend to describe as eccentric. Well, eccentric or not he is now leaping up and down, somewhat alarmingly in my view, in order to flatten a piece of turf along the way. He then recalls, as we pass a particular tree, that on one of his meanders through the gardens he came across a couple of visitors having energetic sex under its boughs. The admission charge for Muncaster does not apparently cover such eventualities.

"Trees," says Patrick, "are like people. I talk to the trees and they respond. Trees are very special because they have rather longer memories than we have, they produce fuel and shelter and they are very beautiful. In this garden if the plants or the trees are not doing well I treat them like people, give them a little haircut and tell them to pull themselves together. What interests me is the link with the people who found the trees and brought them here. The first Lord Muncaster planted most of the big trees in 1783. We have had to start cutting some of the big beeches down because their

shade was getting too much. They were taking too much out of everything round about and it was a wilderness underneath the canopy. The trouble is a lot of the old trees have got past their sell by date now and it's a very great problem but we are planting more trees to replace them."

There are trees from all over the world planted at Muncaster but it is the Spanish chestnut that fascinates me. I have visited the tree many times now and once stood under its boughs in the fading light of a late January afternoon. It had been a brilliant, sharply cold, blue-sky day without a cloud in the sky and the distant fell tops were capped with snow. The tree is deceptively wide and on the surface of its trunk are a series of raised vertical ridges which snake upwards into the higher boughs where there are the tell tale signs of branches being torn off in stormy weather. Below on the grass that January were the spiky husks of chestnuts which fell from the tree in the autumn.

The Spanish chestnut (Castanea sativa) was introduced to this country by the Romans. There was a strong Roman presence in the area and nearby Ravenglass (Glannaventa) was an important naval base in the 2nd Century continuing the defence from Hadrian's Wall south along the coast and inland to Hard Knott and Ambleside.

As the afternoon light faded into evening and I returned to the tree for one last look before heading off for Keswick and home, I was no longer thinking of Thomas Skelton or tomfoolery but was intrigued by the possibility that this lovely old tree in a marvellous location is the progeny, way down the line, of a seed or a sapling that was planted by a homesick foot soldier in a cold and inhospitable land many miles away from the sun and from Rome.

## SCOTS PINE, DERWENTWATER
### On the trail of the lonesome pine
10

On the South Island of New Zealand, where much of the filming took place for *The Lord of The Rings* films, the Milford Trek in fiordland is considered to be 'the finest walk in the world.' Wild and amazing it most certainly is with stretches of beautifully clean rivers full of massive trout, awesome mountain vistas, spectacular waterfalls and fairy tale rainforest. And then there is the plaintive, mournful song of elusive birdlife such as the weka, a cry that brings to mind *The Piano*, directed by Jane Campion, to my mind the single most remarkable movie ever to be filmed in New Zealand and with Michael Nyman's searingly beautiful soundtrack.

Despite its many qualities – and I've been there and walked it – the Milford Trek is not for me the finest walk in the world. The 'for me' is significant because the 'best' of anything is very subjective and to my mind the No1 Walk in the World is, without any doubt, the one that leaves my front door and ends in a bar in Keswick. And, oh yes, I forgot to mention that between door and bar there is some wonderful Lake District scenery and a solitary tree on the shore of Derwentwater, near Hawes End, that deserves a visit if only to acknowledge this particular tree's fortitude. The tree in question is quite literally hanging on in there against all the odds and has done so for many years.

After leaving the sanctuary of my home on Windebrowe Avenue, Keswick, I walk through housing on the outskirts of the town, along Springs Road, through Springs Farm and then, skirting Great Wood (shades of J.R. Tolkien there) up and beyond and onto the gentle slopes of Walla Crag with its fantastic full-value views from the summit out across Derwentwater to Bassenthwaite and the town of Keswick itself resting, as though it has been there for all time, beneath the heather-purple slopes of Skiddaw. The low lying land and the twin lakes, joined at times of extreme flood, are surrounded by the fells: Skiddaw (to your right as you look out over Derwentwater), and then in clockwise direction Blencathra, Helvellyn, Castle Crag, the jaws of Borrowdale, the Scafells, Great Gable, Green Gable and, completing the full 360 degree vista, Maiden Moor, Catbells, Causey Pike, and Grisdale Pike. This would all

Hanging on in there, the Scots Pine near Hawes End, Derwentwater.

make for a fantastic Middle-Earth and if there is a better view on the planet then my name's Ronnie Cape.

From the summit of Walla Crag, where I am in the habit of leaving a little fruit for the ravens that sometimes wait in a bank of nearby firs, I walk out towards Borrowdale. The path curves gently along the fell parallel to Derwentwater and eventually descends to picturesque Ashness Bridge, home to a million photo opportunities. Divvent linger ower lang (don't hang about for ever) at the bridge but walk up the road towards Watendlath, and half a mile or so along leave the tarmac to the right and fork off to a path in Ashness Wood that leads down to Watendlath Beck. Cross a small footbridge and follow the stream up bank to Watendlath and the tarn. It's a beautiful walk alongside the beck and you'll come across a small pine that appears to grow straight out of a rock at the side of the path. Take a slight diversion to the banks of the beck as you approach Watendlath to visit the pool known as the Devil's Punchbowl, a deep circular dub at the foot of a fall in the stream just below where it makes its way through a narrow rocky channel as it begins its descent to Lodore Falls; a cascade that

fails more often than not, unless in high dudgeon, to live up its reputation in Robert
Southey's fun and wordy poem:

*And so never ending, but always descending*
*Sounds and motions for ever and ever are blending*
*All at once and all o'er, with a mighty uproar,*
*And this way the water comes down at Lodore*

The timeless, hanging valley that is Watendlath and its attendant oval shaped tarn,
is the location for part of Sir Hugh Walpole's Herries Chronicle, the novel *Judith Paris*
and its flame-haired heroine. A farm at Watendlath was also home in the 1930s to the
Richardson family (no relation to the author) and the children of the farms there –
Richardsons and Tysons – would make their way in clogs over the fell to Rosthwaite
and school in Borrowdale. Follow in their footsteps over Puddingstone Bank and then
through the village of Rosthwaite ('music ringing through the streets with all those

steel corker clogs on a frosty morning') to the River Derwent where the river is just as beautiful and as cold as the Clinton and Arthur rivers on the Milford Trek. The Derwent – not unlike its colleagues on the other side of the world in New Zealand –

is a river where sunlight on the water brings out the richness of the colour in the stone and slate on the riverbed. The water is as clear as daylight in its purest form without a hint of pollution. Even when the river is in flood it struggles to taint its clarity with mud washed from the banks and the fields on either side.

At Pennybridge Pool (or Pennybrig' as it is known locally) I have watched salmon as they gather in the Autumn to spawn in these pristine waters. And further down the Derwent, at a pool where the water quickens through rocks at Low Hows Wood, I one day saw a cock salmon, lying just to the side of the main current, its bright red skin contrasting vividly in the sunlight with the turquoise of the stones on the river bed. As I edged closer the salmon became aware of my presence and glided smoothly into the deeper water and shelter of the main stream. So utterly captivating was this fleeting encounter with a wild salmon in such a stunning location that this solitary image from the Derwent remains with me and will do so until the lights go out.

This also is the territory of one Millican Dalton, Professor of Adventure of whom you may already have heard. In the summer months he lived in a cave on the side of Castle Crag and among a number of photographs of him there is one where he is attempting to sail his home made raft (don't venture out to the ocean on this) through the waters of the Derwent in the big wide pool just below where I had my encounter with the salmon.

Looking at the Derwent, so peaceful, colourful and at one with the world, it is difficult to imagine that this is one of the headwaters responsible for inflicting flood

and devastation on towns and villages on its route from the fells and lakes to the sea; but more on that later (see chapter 11).

The No 1 Walk in the World (this incidentally is a walk over which you can take as long as you like) now reaches Grange in Borrowdale with its lovely doubled-arched bridge built in 1675. Emerging from the little lane that brings you into Grange take the uphill road to the left and walk along, past the Borrowdale Gates, until another path to your right at Ellers Beck takes you (this is part of The Cumbria Way) towards the head of the lake. From here follow the lakeshore to your left to Great Bay, Myrtle Bay, Otter Island and Brandelhow Bay. Along the way you will have commanding views across the lake to Walla Crag which you climbed earlier.

And yes, we are still on the trail of the lonesome pine and are now rapidly closing in on the tree to which I referred much earlier. Stay with the shore, with the woods to your left. There's also a giant wooden outstretched hand at which to pause – is sculpture really appropriate in a place of such outstanding natural beauty? Just beyond Otterbield Bay and a stone's throw from the Hawes End landing stage – from which I suggest you make the boat journey back across the lake to Keswick and a refreshing drink or three – you will come across The Tree. It is unmistakeable.

Millican Dalton, Professor of Adventure, on his Rogue Herries raft on the Derwent at Borrowdale, a short distance above Grange Bridge.

Ashness Bridge.

Grange Bridge.

Derwentwater from Walla Crag.

If ever there was a tree that clings to life then this is it. The diminutive and decidedly horizontal Scots Pine (Pinus sylvestris) has clearly had a tough time of it. It is a tree that seems to be engaged in an eternal battle for survival. Taut, twisted and stretched out like so much sinew and tendon its exposed roots cling to the land and the shore as though unseen forces are attempting to wrest it from the soil and drag it kicking and

screaming into the lake. This game little tree clings to the planet and to life as though there is no tomorrow. But it has been this way for many years and never looks any different. The little tree's straggly roots are firmly embedded into the edge of the field adjacent to the shore while its trunk, boughs and foliage reach out over the lake and, when the level of the lake is higher than the norm, are partly immersed in the water.

It is as if the tree decided on a hot summer's afternoon to stoop and stretch out over the water for a cooling drink but was then unable to regain the vertical. And so now it has no option but to hang on in there for all time, roots trailing in its wake and uppermost branches pointing out across Derwentwater to Walla Crag and to Blencathra in the distance.

Or perhaps when it was a sapling it was downed in the full force of a tempest and almost torn from the land. So now it lays there, just keeping its head above water for the most part but submerged occasionally at times of flood. Patterns and knobbly bits on parts of its trunk are not unlike barnacles. On other occasions, when the lake is very low, after a prolonged period with only sporadic rainfall, the entire tree, roots and all, is left high and dry on the shore. At times like this it resembles a green-backed spider attempting to crawl its way to the water's edge.

One of the great things about trees is that they can help bring back our childhood. As a lad I was always climbing trees and the temptation to clamber out over the water on the branches of this brave little Scots pine is too much. I cannot resist the call from my boyhood. In this my sixtieth year on the planet I revert to the days when I was six and make my way out over the orange-tinted boughs, peering down into the water below. I stretch out as best I can on a bough and fear that I might never, just like the pine, assume the vertical ever again. But what the hell, this is the Peter Pan in us all. I lie there for a while and stare up through the greenery of the pine needles at the sky and passing clouds. After a while I turn awkwardly onto my belly and peer downwards into the shallow water of the lake, hoping to see minnows, trout, perch or, who knows, perhaps even a jack pike, sliding through the water in search of food or just lying there, impassive, waiting for lunch to come along.

Meanwhile the tree is rooted to the land and all around the timeless fells look down on its struggle to survive.

Previous pages: Sunlight on the water brings out the richness of the colour in the stone and slate on the bed of the River Derwent as it flows through beautiful Borrowdale.

Rosthwaite in all its green Borrowdale finery.

## THE STORM
### A river runs through it

*11*

Val Corbett and I are looking at what used to be a big green field by the River Derwent but which has been transformed into a wasteland of silt, stone and debris. Two oak trees stand defiantly in the midst of this scene of devastation but the force of the flood has toppled a third and its roots are now strung out along the land, like so many telegraph wires after a storm. It was on the night of November 19, 2009 when floodwater twice the height of a man raced like a river through the town centre of Cockermouth and, for a while at least, the world's media spotlight became focused on a small Cumbrian town; a town that at that moment in time joined hands in misfortune with other places around the globe that seem to be increasingly affected by outbursts of extreme weather, flooding and mudslides that bring only misery, death, destruction and worldwide TV images in their wake.

A colourful child's football amid the debris covering a farmer's field by the River Derwent, just below Cockermouth.

Downstream from Cockermouth, trees cast aside by the flood.

Val and I walk across what used to be a field immediately below the Lakes Home Centre on the edge of town. Elsewhere, in fields by the side of the river further down stream, diggers are scooping up mini mountains of stone and debris into spoil heaps ready for wagons to transport them away to goodness knows where. It is unimaginable that all this debris and rock actually came out of the river or was borne along by it. Trees were uprooted and hurled downstream at great speed to be washed up like so much balsa wood in the centre of fields where no tree had previously stood, their upturned trunks pointing accusingly to the sky, now blue and unthreatening. In a cluster of debris near one of the oaks I come across a small, brightly coloured football that provided a stark and poignant contrast to its immediate surroundings. It says it all about man's inferiority when faced by nature's extreme power. Harnessed for energy it is a friendly force, unleashed in a moment of fury and it becomes the enemy, dishing out a lesson.

"It's like a war zone," says Val as she looks incredulously at the scene. "Nature's war zone."

I remember that day / night of the worst of the flooding because I ventured out at its height to see it for myself. In Keswick the River Greta – which joins the River Derwent as it emerges from Borrowdale and Derwentwater at the foot of the lake before heading for Cockermouth, Workington and the Solway – burst its banks and raced through Keswick after rains that were described as of 'biblical proportions' and a 'once in every 1,000 years event.' Torrents of water made our rivers and streams unrecognisable and created havoc on their way from the Lakeland fells to the sea. The flooding at Cockermouth – where the rivers Cocker and Derwent combined forces – was the worst. And there was tragedy at Workington where the River Derwent washed away the massive Northside stone-built road bridge in the middle of the night and claimed the life of a policeman, PC Bill Barker, who was standing on the bridge, preventing other people from venturing onto the bridge after it was discovered that the structure had started to crack. He plunged with the masonry from the bridge into the fast moving water of the river below and was swept away to the sea. His uniformed body was found hours later in the sea at Allonby.

Raging river. On the worst night of the storm the River Greta sped high, wide and ugly under the Wivell Bridge and past the YHA building opposite Fitz Park, Keswick. Photography by Gill Bulch, Keswick.

In the aftermath of the worst of the flooding I could hear the chatter of a helicopter overhead, a familiar sound as hundreds of people were evacuated from their homes in Keswick, Cockermouth and Workington. As night fell the rain lashed relentlessly against the house windows and the wind was shredding the last autumn leaves from the cherry tree in the garden. The prospect was bleak, to say the least.

In Keswick the worst of the rainfall was preceded by the customary restless nights of gale force winds and driving rain – something that has been characteristic of our changing weather patterns in recent years. The River Greta was already bank high when a prolonged period of heavy rain (the wettest since records began in 1766 – 377mm fell in 36 hours at Seathwaite, the wettest inhabited place in England) proved the breaking point and pushed the river not so much over the edge, but into a state no one had witnessed before. If the river was human it would be described as in a blind fury, hell bent on inflicting destruction on anything that stood in its way and, in turn, going out of its way to spread mayhem as far and as wide as possible. There was no holding it back.

This was certainly not the gentle and scenic River Greta by which I have spent many hours walking, fishing, and watching wildlife. The power, force and speed of the river were incredible. I first ventured out at about 8am on the Thursday morning. In judging the height of the water I always take as my first parameter the island in the river at the bottom of Windebrowe Avenue. It was completely covered by the river and provided the first sign that this was something out of the ordinary and not simply the Greta in spate mode. Only the silver birch trees, standing firm against the water, revealed that there was in fact an island there at all.

On that morning I walked over the new Wivell Bridge into Fitz Park, and Peter Towers, of Keswick Parks, was opening the grid mechanism on the 'escape' tunnel to the side of the bridge. Further down stream the water was already starting to wash into the tunnel beneath Station Road where the two parks meet. The water was level with the parapet on the lower park side of the bridge, adjacent to the conker trees. I stood at the water's edge and realised that one slip into the torrent would prove fatal, such was its speed and force. I stood in the lee of the bridge for a while as the rain pelted down and giant waves rolled past, more akin to something you might expect to see on the ocean but certainly not on the beck. At that stage the river had not quite touched the wooden walkway that leads to the youth hostel. Later the walkway became part of the river and further downstream a massive chunk of masonry was sheared from the corner of one of the buildings on Greta Side.

Across the beck from my standpoint near the bridge, a man stood in the light of his flat window and looked out anxiously at the river racing past below. The man at his

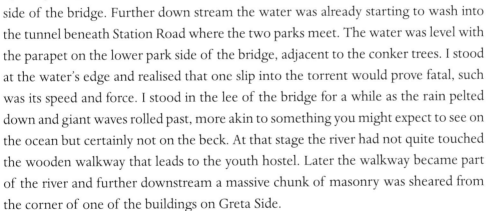

window, a square of bright orange / yellow, provided another meaningful contrast – just like the child's football – to the gloom outside. He looked helpless in the face of the fast-flowing spate river; a metaphor for Man's fallibility when faced by Nature at its most awesome.

I walked on and saw that the river was level with the stone wall just below the footpath that runs parallel to it in Lower Fitz Park. At the windows of houses built next to the river more people looked out of the backs of their homes at the rising water. Further inland on the park the flood had marooned the cricket pavilion and the new football field was virtually under water.

On Crosthwaite Road the river was only a couple of feet at most below the banking that runs alongside the footpath and the road. Although the river was threateningly high there was still no real indication, for me at least, of what was to come in the next few hours with severe flooding, people and homes evacuated, business and sporting premises swamped. And all the distress and repercussions that flooding brings with it. For many people the memory of what happened five years ago was still fresh in their minds. Surely it couldn't happen again? Just when life and their homes had seemingly

returned to normal and measures put in place in the interim would hopefully protect them from a repeat scenario. But for many people living in the less elevated areas of the town and next to the river, heavy rain and a rising beck is a recurring nightmare. It only serves as a painful reminder of the last time their homes and businesses were violated by the water.

Only days before Susan Appleby, the wife of our cricket club President and Treasurer, Edgar, had spoken to me about her fears that they might be flooded for a second time and this only days after they had retired from their book stall on the market and were looking forward to a more leisurely life from the comfort of their home on Crosthwaite Road. Susan was, quite frankly, beside herself with worry and her concern was, sadly, fully justified. Later on that Thursday they had to be evacuated by dinghy from How Keld, leaving their home and possessions – but not Edgar's beloved Wisden collection – to the rising water and its muddy, stinking content.

They were not alone. It was a story that was to be repeated time and again in the immediate area and further afield. There was little or nothing that anyone could do except retreat, keep out of harm's way, do as much as they could to protect life and

Greta Bridge, Keswick.

A torn-up footpath through Lower Fitz Park, Keswick, after the flood.

The old Chinese Bridge, under which the River Derwent normally flows in Borrowdale, with Catbells in the background.

property and wait for the water to relent. Testing times tend to bring out the best in people and, once again, the police, the rescue services, volunteers and the people of the town pulled together. But despite all our technology, brainpower, space travel and the apparent 'superiority' of humans on planet earth, we are quite insignificant when the environment – with which we may irredeemably have tampered – flexes its muscles. Nature inevitably has the final say.

This was far worse than the flooding in January 2005. This was environmental anarchy. Several hours later the transformation was complete and the river had completely flooded the lower part of Keswick. Derwentwater and Bassenthwaite were joined at the hip and many places were impassable or cordoned off. Tons of silt, mud, stone and debris tossed out of the river was strewn over fields and clung to hedgerows and fences. As the light, such as it was, faded into dark and the rain continued to fall, Keswick appeared to be more or less deserted. Police, firemen and volunteers in bright yellow were evident knocking on house doors and warning of the spreading flood as the waters flowed onto Penrith Road and advanced up Greta

Street and the slope towards the war memorial. Police tape across the road barred the way to pedestrians and cars – not that there were many. The occasional car headlights flickered across the river and it was alarming to see the full extent of the flood and its speed.

At Booths store a delivery truck, its lights still flashing, was sinking ever deeper in the waters. From the cab of a van on the town side of Greta Bridge, two yellow-jacketed men prevented anyone from venturing onto the bridge itself. The fear was that it might collapse, one of many bridges in the county that were closed until their strength or otherwise could be determined after supports were eroded by the torrent.

Daylight brought home the full impact of the flood. Once again the lower Fitz Park footpath that runs along the river had been ripped up and deposited many yards away, like so many layers of carpet, on the old football field.

One section of tarmac, in what would normally have been a goalmouth, was in the form of a spiral or upside down cone. From a distance I thought it must be mud or silt. Close examination showed that it was tarmac, twisted and formed into a strange sculpture.

And the people of Keswick, and many others elsewhere in the stricken towns and villages of Cumbria, began the long, soul destroying process of putting their livelihoods, their homes and their lives together again.

This rain, almost monsoon like, the high winds that invariably accompany the rain, and the flooding that we are increasingly having to endure in Lakeland and in Keswick all smack of climate change. There are, of course, many people who remain sceptical but evidence points to Man and our pollution being to blame for what is happening

now, not just here in Lakeland but all over Planet Earth and in many different forms, whether it's the icecaps melting, excessive heat, rain, storms, or the burning sun scorching through holes in the ozone layer.

We appear to be reaping the whirlwind and will continue to do so unless World governments unite and get serious in trying to deal with the threat to our environment. It may not be too late, but all the warning signs are quite clearly there. For me it's the sight of a twisted spiral of tarmac emerging out of a playing field in Fitz Park where only blades of grass should be. Or a brightly-coloured child's football among the debris of rock, stone and silt where once there was a farmer's field by the river and where cattle would graze or stand calf-deep in the shallows of the river to stay cool on a hot summer's day.

The flooded River Derwent below Portinscale with Skiddaw beyond.

# WIND BLOWN HAWTHORN
## Desolation Island

*12*

When I was a lad, nine years old, wearing short trousers and climbing trees at every opportunity, one of the proudest and, for that matter, surprising moments in my early life – as I did not think of myself as being particularly academic, in fact I believed I was reasonably thick – was to be awarded a prize at junior school. It came right out of the blue. I was in Standard 2 at the time, taught by a smashing man called Ken Robinson and the citation, on a label stuck to the inside cover of my prize, reads: 'Brigham School, Keswick. Awarded to Keith Richardson for Progress, Standard II, 22 July, 1959.' The prize, which I have alongside me on the desk as I write, was a medium sized, 221-page, hard backed book, bound in a light red and entitled *The Ship Aground*.

The book's author was C (Cicely) Fox Smith and was illustrated by C Walter Hodges. It is an adventure story, set in the 18th Century, published by the Oxford Children's Library (The Oxford University Press), and to this day remains a proud possession and one that continues to conjure up wonderful images and thoughts of the sea, sailing ships, anchors, wharfs, mariners, pirates, harbour side inns, rum, seagulls, cliffs . . . in fact the whole damn beautiful and ugly brine of the ocean and all who sail on her.

The opening page has a lovely black and white line drawing of The Ship Aground, a fictional inn on the Thames in Wapping, and Chapter 1, under the heading 'In which I make the Acquaintance of Captain Cross Bones' begins: "I well remember the first day I set eyes on my Uncle Ben Strange . . ."

The central character of the book, an orphan by the name of Barty Dale, is kidnapped from his uncle's inn, The Ship Aground, and forced to crew a ship that sails to the other side of the world. Pirates, mutiny, shipwreck and survival on an island called Desolation are all part of the adventure that ensues. It's so wonderfully *Treasure Island* and is very Jim lad, aye! But loses none of its appeal for all that.

The book ends with the paragraph: "I have sailed many seas since all this happened, and seen many lands; but never again have I set eyes on Desolation Island – on its high central peak wrapped in a wisp of cloud, and its barren slopes where the homeless

'The Ship Aground' illustration by C Walter Hodges from the book of that title published by Oxford University Press.
© Image courtesy of the estate of C Walter Hodges.

Hawthorn in blossom on Humphrey Head.

Overleaf: Standing in the face of adversity. Windblown hawthorn on Humphrey Head.

wind blows forever, and its cliffs at whose feet the broad Pacific shatters endlessly in foam."

The book smacks of the sea in a big way and while I, personally, have never ventured greatly onto the oceans (apart, that is, from the Cook Strait between New Zealand's North and South islands and the Caribbean between Tobago and Trinidad) I do appreciate the sea and all that it has brought to our island home over the years and no more so than here in Cumbria where the coastline is rich in nautical history and the ports of Whitehaven and Maryport once played a major role in trade and shipbuilding, and particularly in the 19th Century. Nowadays the harbour town of Whitehaven is increasingly significant as a tourist destination with its attractive marina, Georgian architecture, the magnificent piers reaching out, a left hand finger and thumb-like pincer movement into the Irish Sea, and the nearby Beacon museum where there are displays and an amazing collection, including archive paintings, relating to the town's maritime and industrial history.

Maryport, also, has developed along similar lines and all along the Cumbrian coast there are great locations to explore and to feel the full aura of the sea and all that it represents, as far as the eye can travel to the horizon and as far back in time as the mind's eye will take you. If you have the imagination the sea will do the rest.

My journey up the coast starts at Morecambe Bay on a whale-backed promontory of limestone called Humphrey Head that has the most amazing specimens of wind blown hawthorn on its higher reaches. These defiant little trees are evocative of the sea. Not unlike sailors down the centuries whose minds and limbs have been moulded by the impact of a life on the ocean wave, the coastal hawthorn has been shaped by the salt-laden elements and gale force winds blasting the shoreline. No respite given or taken. No other landlocked object bears as great a visual testimony to the power of the sea – no eroded cliff or debris-strewn beach – as the hawthorn trees on Humphrey Head. They are works of art, carved and shaped like old men bent over and walking into the wind, trunk and branches cruelly and unrelentingly forged and gnarled by the elements that hit them from the first day that they lifted their heads above the turf and rock of the headland; troopers popping their heads above the soil, scrub and rock, only to be twisted over from birth, like pieces of iron hammered into distorted shapes on the anvil that is Humphrey Head with the sea wind its bellows. And then, after the worst of winter's blows, 'death' by hundreds of years of extreme exposure, the hawthorn somehow blossoms into life with its wonderful top decking of white flowers, gently massaged by warm summer breezes and coastal sunshine. It is as though the sea is licking the wounds of its victim after winter has done its damnedest to inflict pain and suffering.

Why, of all places, did the hawthorn choose to grow here? Or was it simply a case of it being the only tree hardy enough to survive on a headland where everything else would perish at the first blast? As I stand under the boughs of a wind blown hawthorn, its branches trailing out behind me like the tail of a gabardine on an upside down man, I discover that it is actually windier directly under the tree than it is outside the span of its branches. It is almost as though the hawthorn is a magnet for the wind and where it funnels through its branches and around its trunk it blows stronger, outside it is almost still and a great deal quieter.

It occurs to me that the hawthorn must love the wind and that the 'feeling' is reciprocated. One of the trees has been reduced to a single and very thin trunk, more like a branch. Little more than the thickness of your wrist it clings precariously to the limestone and gives the impression that it could be borne away at any moment.

Wisps of sheep's wool are attached to the base of another tree and to the strand of barbed wire against the dry stone wall that skirts the flank of the headland. At one point, rather unusually, a five-barred yat provides a gateway and a window to the sea. It is a gate that does not appear to have any fixed purpose and yet it does not look out of place, quite the contrary. I like the appearance of a good, solid yat in the countryside. It seems to frame the view beyond and provides a welcome, an open door to the vista.

The walk over the head is a gentle one along a spine of limestone interspersed with grass, scrub and, on closer examination at ground level, little bright yellow flowers tinged with red / orange. After reaching the highest point, with Humphrey Head's cliffs to the west, you can follow the fence line down to the shore where the limestone of the head meets the sands of Morecambe Bay and where, on my visit, a flock of sheep and lambs was making its way around the point to feeding grounds on the salt

Ravenglass, the estuary and the
view from the sea.

marsh. The views from Humphrey Head are superb with the Lakeland fells at your back as you look out to sea and around you to Lancaster and Morecambe. Wind turbines paddle up to their knees in the water on the horizon. Across the Levens estuary to Ulverston the distinctive Hoad monument on the hill is clearly visible. Ulverston was, of course, the birthplace of Stan Laurel and I have a mental picture of a young Stan, still looking faintly perplexed at life, making his way up Hoad Hill to the monument. This would be long before he made it big with his partner in laughter Oliver Hardy in Hollywood and, specifically, the Blue Ridge Mountains of Virginia where they famously embarked on the trail of the lonesome pine. Who could possibly forget Laurel and Hardy at their best? Leaning against a bar in the movie *Way Out West* and singing along to a cowboy on a guitar with that wonderful chorus:

*In the Blue Ridge Mountains of Virginia,*
*On the trail of the lonesome pine—*
*In the pale moonshine our hearts entwine,*
*Where she carved her name and I carved mine;*
*Oh, June, like the mountains I'm blue—*
*Like the pine I am lonesome for you,*
*In the Blue Ridge Mountains of Virginia,*
*On the trail of the lonesome pine.*

The one blot on the landscape as you look out from Humphrey Head is the ugly rectangular block that is Heysham Power Station – another fine mess – directly across the bay. There is also a lot to see closer at hand with peregrines swooping across the cliffs and climbing high before descending, wings tight to the body like scimitars, to take out an unsuspecting pigeon at high speed.

An information board at the pathway entrance to the head tells you that it is owned by the Holker Estate and has been managed by Cumbria Wildlife Trust since 1992. It is also known as the Joy Ketchen Nature Reserve in memory of the trust's first conservation officer. The head is rich in fossils and the carboniferous rock was formed on the bed of a shallow sea 325 million years ago, give or take a year or two.

Apart from the striking nature of the wind blown hawthorn, the head is blessed with an abundance of wildlife and plant life and is visited regularly by the lesser spotted Twitcher person who will delight in telling you that the pigeon killed by a falcon was then finished off – after the falcon had enjoyed the best part of the meal – by two ravens.

It is claimed that Humphrey Head was the location for the slaughter in the 15th Century of the last wolf in England; the weather vane on nearby Cartmel Priory depicts a wolf's head. However, many other places in the UK make similar boasts and I would treat each and every one of them with a pinch of salt. The stories tend to be heavily romanticised and usually involve gentry on horseback with hounds, long chases and much derring-do.

Further north up the coast I am always attracted to the port of Ravenglass. It is a magical seaside village with an intriguing main street and it always seems to me as if it is a place of fantasy, as though it cannot possibly be real and has been put on this planet as a perpetual film set. But Ravenglass is real enough and – because of its strong Roman connections – I never have any difficulty in looking out towards the estuary where the rivers Esk, Irt and Mite all merge and imagine the curved prow, sail and oars of a Roman galley making its way majestically upstream for a place to berth.

Ravenglass dates back to the 2nd Century and was known by the Romans as Glannoventa. It had a garrison of 500 soldiers and was the beginning of a Roman supply chain linking the sea to the land and extending up Eskdale and over Hardknott Pass to Ambleside and beyond.

Today one of the catamarans anchored in the estuary and holding firm against the strong flow of the Esk is Frank Chamberlain's bright yellow *Lady Primrose*. One still and beautiful sunlit evening in 2007 I went out with Frank in his catamaran on a lobster

fishing expedition. I quickly realised that you do not fully appreciate Ravenglass's unique position in the world until you have seen it from the vantage point of a boat out at sea, with the Lakeland fells stretching beyond the shore and village. Frank described Ravenglass as "a lost world" and I know precisely what he meant. Nowhere else smacks so much of the sea and all things nautical, marine and deeply historical; it is a place cast adrift in time.

On the seaward side of the main street, a washing line distance from the backs of the houses, upright poles stand at jaunty angles in the mud, silt and pebbles in which they are embedded. And when they are used as washing lines and the sheets and shirts billow and flap wildly like sails in the sea breeze of a summer's day it provides the iconic image of this ancient West Cumbrian port of call. In a darker vein you could almost imagine a blonde sacrificial victim, all tears and entreaties, chained to a pole to await a fate worse than death in the jaws of some terrible creature from the deep that must, periodically, be appeased by an offering of flesh and blood.

Quaint old steps lead up to the backs of the houses. The lobster fisherman's pots are stacked high against the back of his house – there's a small boat to the front – and atop them are his marker flags, black and gold. Nearby is an abandoned anchor, rusted to hell but resolute. Nothing, it would seem, is going to shift this old heavyweight from its final resting place. It is like an old sea salt, retired at last and able to spend his final days staring out to sea. The sounds as well as the sights here are all of the sea, with something metallic clanking regularly in the rigging of a catamaran competing with the screeching chatter of a sandpiper as it lands to search for food along the shoreline.

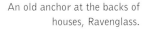
An old anchor at the backs of houses, Ravenglass.

A stroll along the main street of the village is a pleasant excursion in itself and I like the way the street and its walls narrow significantly as you approach the end of the tarmac where two big iron gates are folded on either side ready to guard against flooding. This narrow juncture makes the view beyond all the more impressive and it explodes on your vision with the fast moving curve of the Esk in the immediate foreground and the hulk that is Black Combe in the distance.

Such is the maritime charm and magic of Ravenglass that to see a mermaid here would not be such a great surprise.

Nine sea shells, the largest of them old and grey and conch-like in appearance and size, and two of them freshly pink and relatively new and much smaller, flat and fan–like in shape, sit on a gravestone in the churchyard of the Priory Church of St Mary and St Bega, St Bees (dedicated in 1125). The shells appear to be strategically placed and rest on the three-tiered plinth that rises up to the pillar of the headstone. The older of the shells have possibly been there since the grave was dug. The grave is known locally as 'The Sailors' Grave' and in it are the bodies, in three rows of four, of 12 mariners. Eleven of them are Italian seamen, names not known, while the twelfth is one Henry Legg, an English deep-sea pilot from Falmouth in Cornwall. How did they come to be there?

The inscription on the grave reads:
IN CHRIST
HENRY LEGG DEEP SEA PILOT
AND XI MARINERS OF THE
BARQUE LUIGI OLIVARI
XII JANUARY MDCCCLXXIX

The sea shell-bedecked grave of the mariners of the Luigi Olivari in the graveyard at The Priory Church of St Mary and St Bega, St Bees.

It transpires that the barque, the *Luigi Olivari*, was taking grain from Philadelphia to Silloth in January 1879 when it ran aground off Braystones. A boy, John McGill, aged 11, and who lived at the Braystones railway station, believed he fleetingly saw (presumably through a window) a ship's mast-light in the dark. It was an atrocious night with snow falling and a gale force wind blowing in off the sea. He was sure that the light was too close to shore. He told his mother, but when she looked there was nothing to be seen and felt he must have been mistaken.

The next morning revealed that the boy had been right. The shore below the railway station was strewn with wreckage and when Maria McGill, the boy's mother, went out she saw bodies among the rocks. Searchers found eight bodies and a further four were washed up at St Bees Beach and at Fleswick Bay further north along the coast. The first eight bodies were laid out on straw in a stable in St Bees where an inquest was subsequently held. The corpses were not a pretty sight, some were mutilated and one had no arms or legs, most of its head was missing and the body disembowelled.

Henry Legg's body was identified from his pilot's certificate in a tin in his pocket. The others were given numbers and all were later buried together in the churchyard at St Bees. Meanwhile local police were called in to stop locals taking clothes and other goods washed ashore from the wreck. A week after the funeral the salvage from the wreck was auctioned on the beach. Timber, chain, anchors and much of the original cargo fetched about £450.

The young boy, John (or Jack) McGill, who first saw the Luigi Olivari in trouble,

All at sea. A grounded trawler
at Fleswick Beach.

Golden light.
Seascale from the sea.

went to sea when he grew up and left a widow and three daughters at Sea View, St Bees, when he was drowned in 1903 after his ship sank in a hurricane off Florida.

It is difficult to picture the scene of the auction of the salvage from the *Luigi Olivari* as I enjoy an ice cream on the promenade at St Bees on a lovely summer's day some 130 years later. I walk out along the shore and climb the slope that leads onto St Bees Head, making my way past the anchor of the Spanish steamer the *Izaro* that came to grief in thick fog just below Tomlin in 1907 with the crew scrambling to safety as the ship was stranded on the rocks.

Swallows cut the air along the path as they swoop and glide spectacularly for food on the wing. On gaining higher ground I step out to the edge of the cliff and below is the shape of the old swimming pool, no possible use now for bathing as the sea has filled it with rocks and silt. The pool was dynamited and cut into the sandstone on the rocky headland below Tomlin in the 1930s, a project for the local unemployed of the depression era.

My destination is Fleswick Bay, a cove that looks as if it was specially made for smugglers bringing French brandy into the country. The field slopes gently down to a cut in the land that opens onto the beach itself. To your left as you face the sea is the expanse of the stony beach and on either side the towering sandstone cliffs of St Bees Head on which fulmars, guillemots, razorbills, cormorants, kittiwakes and herring gulls nest. The tide is going out and at the water's edge the rocks are lime green with a light covering of seaweed while further out they are the tangled darker green / brown of kelp. A few large

sandstone boulders on the beach stand out, big brothers in the shingle that shifts and sinks beneath your feet as you walk.

Three heavy pieces of rusted machinery, presumably the remains of a trawler – the largest chunk of machinery is quite clearly winching gear – are grafted to the shore. Rocks, seaweed and shells have invaded and claimed them. The sun is bright and strong and a speedboat bounces across the sea towards Whitehaven up the coast and leads the eye to a solitary angler on the rocks to the north of the bay. He hurls his line far out to sea, the trace whizzing off the multiplier reel and given impetus by the heavy lead weight at the end. The angler then reels and draws it back in, hoping

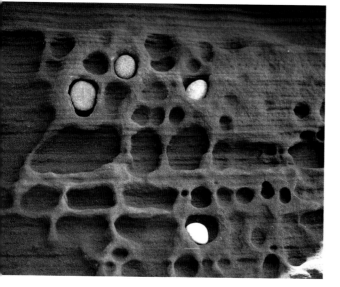

to hook a mackerel or two and possibly more on the multi-coloured feathers he is using as lures. Fresh out of the water the mackerel is a beautiful fish, a shiny-wet blue-green with maize-like curved black lines on its back and a silver underbelly. It is a fighter as well as a predator and it's sad to see a fish thrashing around for life in the confines of an angler's plastic bag, its energy fading and the death throes becoming less intense as life ebbs away. Far better had it been knocked on the head and put out of its misery.

Closer examination of the shore reveals wonderful wave-like patterns in the rock and little pools that have their very own miniature art exhibitions of a few colourful pebbles and a sprig of seaweed. Nature's art is always the best; far better certainly than the names, dates and shapes crudely carved into the lower reaches of the sandstone cliffs together with the occasional profound observation (not) such as: 'UFO. The truth is out there . . .' It doubtless is, but I don't need to be reminded of the fact on a slab of sandstone in a secluded cove where the sea is god and nature always reminds you of its presence.

I recall a news story that appeared in the pages of a local newspaper, a report on an inquest. If my memory is correct a young man had been walking the coast in this area looking for crabs in rock pools. He had failed to return home one evening and was found drowned in a shallow pool the following morning. A knife lay nearby and it appeared that he had attempted to cut his hand free. There was evidence of a deep bite mark on the right hand and it was concluded that as he searched for crabs among the rock pools a conger eel, wrapped around a rock, had grabbed him by the fingers and held on. As the tide came in the increasingly desperate young man failed in his attempt to cut himself free of the conger and drowned.

While the coast is undoubtedly beautiful it is clearly also a very dangerous place. Even on a sunny day in midsummer you are not entirely safe on the stony beach at Fleswick Bay. On the occasion of my last visit I was dive bombed by gulls. I had been aware of a sudden flicker of wings and a retort in the air above me but was blissfully oblivious to any threat. So much so that I did not think much of it. Then it dawned on me what was happening and as I looked up to the very top of the cliff, hundreds of feet above, I saw a gull standing near its nest, presumably with chicks. It opened its wings and took off, like a diver from a high board, arcing its way in an impressive loop towards me on the beach, only pulling out of its dive at the last moment and spiralling upwards. I got the message and moved on.

St Bees beach from the headland.

The waves have created this unique pattern in the stone on Fleswick Bay.

Part of Whitehaven's Maritime Festival, somewhat incongruously perhaps, is a massive fun fair. The area off the West Pier, on the car park overlooking the Solway below the Candlestick chimney, has been invaded by glitzy and gaudy rides and side shows including two with an American connection. These have an added significance to me now because during the American Revolutionary War, John Paul Jones (originally from Kirkcudbright, apprenticed aboard a ship out of Whitehaven as a boy of 13 and who subsequently emigrated to America) was captain of the USS Ranger that attacked the West Cumbrian port where his life at sea began. On the night of April 23, 1778, he spiked the port's guns on the Half Moon Battery but failed in his bid to set fire to the 200 - 400 wooden ships anchored in the harbour. On the parking area above Tom Hurd's Rock below the south beach is the black bulk of a cannon known as 'Long Tom'. The gun was recovered from near to Tom Hurd's rock in 1963 and was one of the guns spiked by John Paul Jones. On the day when I visited, the car park was taken over by a 21st Century fun fair – complete with ranks of cuddly white tiger prizes – and I find it mildly amusing that Whitehaven and its maritime festival is once again being 'invaded' by America, in the shape of two rides called Superbowl and Planet Hollywood.

No less curious is the proximity of all this fun and games to the Candlestick chimney that originally provided ventilation for the old Wellington Pit (sunk in 1840 and closed in 1932). The castellated building with its keep and turrets near the chimney was the entrance to the colliery which, like others in the area, were at one time owned and run by the Lowther family.

And while they provided employment for the area and commerce for the town and port it all came at a price. Wellington Pit was the site of Whitehaven's worst mining disaster in 1910 when an explosion of gas and subsequent fires resulted in the loss of 136 miners, men and boys.

Loss of life was not limited to the mines that stretched out many miles under the sea (Saltom Pit, sunk in 1729 was the first under sea coal mine). The West Cumbrian coast also claimed lives at sea, as can be seen from the earlier reference to the *Luigi Olivari*. The first recorded shipwreck off the Cumbrian coast was in 1299 when the *Holy Cross* was washed ashore near Silloth. There were many more and extensive records for the years 1807 – 1866 show, for example, that the brig *Richardson*, out of Debtford, perished at Saltom Bay with seven lives lost and in 1816 the 209-ton ship *Rose* was wrecked on Tom Hurd's Rock, the latter situated immediately below the Candlestick on Whitehaven's south shore.

Tom Hurd's Rock got its name from a tragic story. In the late 18th Century the coastal village of Parton, just north of Whitehaven, was an important port in its own right. It was also popular with young people who would sail or row to the village before returning to Whitehaven on the ebb tide. Tom Hurd himself was a sailor and served in the Royal Navy during the reign of William IV. The sea was calm when Tom, his fiancé, Eliza, and her brother, set off from Whitehaven for Parton. They spent the afternoon at an inn but the weather changed. In a dramatic and colourful account, documented in the local newspaper *The Whitehaven News*, the story unfolds: 'Towards the middle of the day the sky darkened. The wind veered, in a short space of time, to every point of the compass. Huge threatening clouds, gathering in the north, gave every indication of a coming tempest.'

Perhaps the party and the young men in particular were full of bravado, fortified by drink and determined to return to Whitehaven by the same route even though

'the sea was greatly agitated, swelling and heaving and emitting that deep ominous sound which is the unfailing prognostic of a coming storm. Fierce gusts of wind had already begun to crest the top of the waves, which roared as they rolled onwards and broke upon the shore at last on a tumultuous mass of foam.' The storyteller was clearly warming to the task.

Eliza was in the stern as the two men pushed off from the quay and set sail for Whitehaven.

'Both men kept steadily at the oars until the wind changed in their favour, veering to the north east. Their progress was such that a safe and speedy end to their perilous voyage seemed certain. But then the hurricane came on like a tornado and the waves, lashed as they were into torture by the blast, raged and roared and tossed the boat from their bosoms.'

Even so they had almost reached the harbour mouth when Tom Hurd's oar was snapped in two and the boat was 'driven along like a cork on the water and, to the dismay of those collected on the quays, was carried with fearful rapidity across the mouth of the harbour' where it was dashed against the rock. One of the men was seen clinging to the rock and 'after many desperate efforts he succeeded in reaching the topmost ledge. It was Hurd, closely clasping with his left arm the apparently lifeless body of his intended bride . . . hour after hour did Hurd sit upon the fatal rock holding the body of Eliza while the waves raged around them.'

Seamen were eventually able to reach the rock as the tide retreated and 'they found

The two piers at Whitehaven.

Paintings depicting Whitehaven's seafaring past. Images courtesy of The Beacon and Copeland Borough Council.

Hurd sitting in a state of insensibility, still holding his loved one close to his breast, with his cold cheek against hers that was already fixed in the rigidity of death. It was a sight that might have drawn tears from the most insensible heart that ever beat in the human breast.'

The body of Eliza's brother was later washed ashore.

The story, however, does not end there. Hurd, clearly badly affected by the tragedy, may have felt entirely responsible for what happened. In his grief and guilt he took to wandering along the shore and would sit for hours upon the rock, in fair weather or foul, as the tidal water surrounded him and then receded. The inconsolable young man continued his almost daily pilgrimage to the rock until, in the winter of the following year, his friends discovered that he was missing following a particularly severe storm. They found his lifeless body in a small cavity worn into the cliff by the tide. And the rock, which ultimately claimed his life, also granted him immortality when it became known as Tom Hurd's Rock.

It is far from easy to gain access to Tom Hurd's Rock these days. Cliff top fencing cuts you off from the pebble beach that is situated below higher land that is crumbling and unstable. Warning signs tell you repeatedly of the danger. I managed to clamber down to the beach with some difficulty and made my way out to the rock at low tide. It is an unspectacular hunk of rock, hard and uncompromising and to be dashed against its flanks by an onrushing tide could doubtless prove fatal; as it did for Tom Hurd's fiancé.

Tom Hurd's Rock, Whitehaven.

175

Sailing into the wide blue yonder. A fishing boat in full sail leaves Maryport.

Gravestones with a maritime significance in a Maryport churchyard.

The Maryport-built Peter Iredale in its final resting place on the Oregon coast, USA, where it is now a major tourist attraction. The ship ran aground on October 25, 1906. Picture by Gary Randall. www.gary-randall.com

Val Corbett's image of a sailing ship about to leave Maryport harbour for the open sea of the Solway Firth is timeless. It also brings to mind the countless ships, built at Maryport in the days when the town, together with Whitehaven, Workington and Harrington further down the coast, had a considerable reputation for shipbuilding. Many of these vessels travelled the world and some ended their days as shipwrecks in distant corners of the planet, hit by icebergs off Cape Horn, torpedoed by German submarines, sunk by mines, or some other unknown fate, lost without trace and, in some instances, all hands lost.

Of those to sail out of Maryport, for example, *The Peter Iredale* (1890), a four-masted steel barque en route to Portland, Oregon, came to grief in thick mist and a squall on the Clatsop Spit sands at the mouth of the Columbia River on October 25, 1906. To this day the wreck rises eerily out of the sands and is a tourist attraction in Clatsop County, Oregon. It is one of the most accessible shipwrecks of the 'Graveyard of the Pacific,' and the rudder is situated in the parking lot of the Columbia River Maritime Museum in nearby Astoria. Captain H Lawrence's final toast to his stricken ship was: "May God bless you, and may your bones bleach in the sands."

All hands were saved when *The Peter Iredale* perished on the sands. Many others were not so fortunate, including the 22-man crew of *The Midas*, built by Ritson and Co at Maryport in 1896 and which made her maiden voyage out of Maryport on August 3, 1897, bound for Nagasaki with a cargo of steel rails. *The Midas* was lost with all hands en route from Nagasaki to Portland and was last heard of on February 14, 1898. The unfortunate crew, mostly out of Maryport, consigned to the fish, crabs, eels and the elements of the deep.

Maryport Aquarium, situated alongside the quay from which the town's ships left the harbour, many never to return, is a surprising place. What I certainly did not expect to find was a wooden sculpture, from the Pitcairn Islands, of a flying fish. The fish was apparently carved out of timber taken from the hull of *The Bounty*. It provides an interesting link with Fletcher Christian who was born and raised inland from Maryport before making his famous journey aboard *The Bounty* with Captain William Bligh and ending up on the Pitcairn Islands where he and the rest of the mutineers went native.

178

In sharp contrast to this unusual wooden exhibit at the aquarium are the real and very beautiful fish, the metallic silver of the gilthead bream; the almost psychedelic colouring and patterns of the dragonet, gold on white with a hint of red around the jaw; anemones of many colours and swirling tentacles; a luminous tiny sand smelt; the bright pink sunstar starfish; the amazingly camouflaged Dover sole which changes its colour to its immediate environment; the soft white coral that is dead man's fingers; the thornback ray, the smooth hound spotted ray and the lesser spotted dogfish in the larger fish tank; the small bright orange fish, angel fish in shape, segmented by striking white bands enclosed in thick black lines and always, always on the move, this way and that; the long thin pipe fish and its dart-like tail;  and a spectacular shrimp with a red back along which runs a vivid white stripe.

All these and many more introduce you to the wonders of the sea and marine life but there was one exhibit, the smallest, that stopped me dead. These were the dwarf seahorses. So tiny, only two centimetres tall at best, so fragile and so heart-stoppingly beautiful in their vulnerability as they rode serenely across the water or

clung tentatively to bright green strands of eel grass. While the dwarf sea horse is small it had a massive effect upon me as I gazed on its miniature world. This, after all, is its universe, a small fish tank in an aquarium, situated on the harbour side of a West Cumbrian port, leagues away from its natural home in the Bahamas or in the sea off the USA. And beyond that there is the horizon and thousands of miles of ocean that they will never know, the currents of the deep and the stars and the moon above in the black of the night sky and its many planets, other worlds that are light years away.

Looking into the fish tank containing the seahorse is like looking in a mirror. You see your self, so small and insignificant in the enormity of the universe and in the face of everything we don't know or even begin to understand.

Outside in the sunshine I sit on a bench on the side of the harbour, just beyond where the River Ellen makes its final freshwater rush over the shallows to the sea. I eat fish and chips from The Cross Quays chippie across the harbour and watch my world go by. A herring gull perches on the wall and waits impatiently for a feed from my lunch, aggressively strutting his stuff and chasing off any other would-be interlopers, including a sorry looking pigeon with cat gut entwined around its legs.

Across the other side of the bridge that leads to the harbour area the maritime museum is closed but outside, on the far side of the road and looking down over the

Dwarf seahorse in Maryport Aquarium.

Harbourside at Maryport with nets and trawlers.

Looking out across the Solway to Scotland.

'The Fishy Tale' sculpture at Maryport by Colin Telfer.

Ellen, is a sculpture *A Fishy Tale* by Colin Telfer. Two men, one presumably a trawler man recently returned from the sea and with a basket of fish at his feet, and the other a local leaning forward with interest, are engaged in conversation while a boy with a dog look on, the dog apparently intrigued by the fish.

I walk out to the pier where a solitary sea angler casts his line from the heights of the wall far out into the incoming tide and a swallow zips back and forward among the pier supports. On the other side of the Solway wind turbines stand in line in the sea.

It is all a far cry from the time when sailing ships built on this coast would leave the harbours of their homeland for foreign waters. But if you half close your eyes it is not difficult to picture the scene and imagine the sounds of another century, the heyday of the 19th and before that. In many respects a hell of a lot has changed since then; in others very little has altered.

Through it all, as I take in the atmosphere of the quay and the Solway at Maryport on a summer's afternoon, I am always tempted to look back rather than forward; to a time when the sea and people who sailed on her out of ports just like this somehow had a great deal more romance about them than is now the case. It would doubtless be a harder life, more demanding in many ways, but setting out to sea in a sailing ship, destined for a foreign land on the other side of the world, was a very real adventure.

And this feeling for the sea takes me back to the wind blown hawthorn on Humphrey Head and to my childhood and the book *The Ship Aground* and its significance in framing my feelings about the sea and its romance.

And from there it leads me, finally, to a very fine poem by Cicely Fox Smith, author of *The Ship Aground*, that strikes a ship's bell.

### A Ship in a Bottle

*In a sailormen's restaurant Rotherhithe way,*
*Where the din of the docksides is loud all the day,*
*And the breezes come bringing off basin and pond*
*And all the piled acres of lumber beyond,*
*From the Oregon ranges the tang of the pine*
*And the breath of the Baltic as bracing as wine …*
*Among the stale odours of hot food and cold,*
*In a fly-spotted window I there did behold*
*A ship in a bottle some sailor had made*
*In watches below, swinging South with the Trade,*
*When the fellows were patching old dungaree suits,*
*Or mending up oilskins and leaky sea-boots,*
*Or whittling a model, or painting a chest,*
*Or smoking and yarning and watching the rest.*

*In fancy I saw him — all weathered and browned,*
*Deep crows'-feet and wrinkles his eyelids around,*
*A pipe in the teeth that seemed little the worse*
*For Liverpool pantiles and stringy salt horse …*
*The hairy forearm with its gaudy tattoo*
*Of a bold-looking female in scarlet and blue …*
*The fingers all roughened and toughened and scarred,*
*With hauling and hoisting so calloused and hard,*
*So crooked and stiff you would wonder that still*
*They could handle with cunning and fashion with skill*
*The tiny full-rigger predestined to ride*
*To its cable of thread on its green-painted tide,*
*In its wine-bottle world while the old world went on,*
*And the sailor who made it was long ago gone.*

*And still as he worked at the toy on his knee*
*He would spin his old yarns of the ships and the sea,*
*Thermopylae, Lightning, Lothair and Red Jacket,*
*And many another such famous old packet —*
*And many a tough bucko and daredevil skipper*

*In Liverpool blood-boat and Colonies clipper —*
*The sail that they carried aboard the Black Ball,*
*Their skysails and stunsails and ringtail and all,*
*And storms that they weathered, and races they won,*
*And records they broke in the days that are done.*

*Or else he would sing you some droning old song,*
*Some old sailor's ditty both mournful and long,*
*With queer little curleycues, twiddles and quavers,*
*Of smugglers and privateers, pirates and slavers,*
*'The Brave Female Smuggler', the 'packet of fame'*
*That sails from New York, an' the "Dreadnought's her name",*
*And "All on the coast of the High Barbaree",*
*And "The flash girls of London were the downfall of he".*

*In fancy I listened, in fancy could hear*
*The thrum of the shrouds and the creak of the gear,*
*The patter of reef-points on tops'ls a-shiver,*
*The song of the jibs when they tauten and quiver,*
*The cry of the frigate-bird following after,*
*The bow-wave that broke with a gurgle like laughter:*
*And I looked on my youth with its pleasure and pain,*
*And the shipmate I loved was beside me again …*
*In a ship in a bottle a-sailing away*
*In the flying-fish weather through rainbows of spray,*
*Over oceans of wonder by headlands of gleam*
*To the harbours of youth on the wind of a dream!*

**Cicely Fox Smith**

This poem was first published in *Punch* magazine in September 1920 and subsequently in a collection entitled *Ship Models* published by Conway Maritime Press in 1972.

It is a bitterly cold evening and the wind is blowing straight out of the far north. The United Kingdom, in an image from a satellite orbiting the earth, resembles an Arctic wasteland. It is early December and the country is icicle-cold with sub zero temperatures well into double figures. Schools are closed, some roads are impassable and film on the television news is full of people shuffling and skittering about like penguins on ice. It is the sort of day that will freeze you to the core of your being. In the shelter of the tree cracked and bone dry leaves, like small pieces of discarded parchment, scurry this way and that on the wind and over the snow. The leaves are like ghosts of the glorious Autumn just departed and refuse to pass on to the other side unless, that is, someone sweeps them up into a bonfire and releases their souls on a cloud of pungent leaf smoke to the woodland in the sky.

I, too, might resemble a ghost. As the light starts to fade I find myself wandering among the snow-capped gravestones of The Parish Church of St Michael in the centre of the Lowther estate, near Penrith. There is no one else about, certainly not living. A passer-by might mistake me for an undertaker on a recce or a rector on a mission, garbed as I am in a long, flowing, wind-blown navy blue overcoat, black trousers, black woollen gloves, black scarf – it wasn't my intention to be so black – and clutching a black book. It could be a Bible but it is, in fact, a notebook.

Jack's Yak at Lowther. Note the bough held aloft by wooden props.

The mausoleum at St Michael's Church, Lowther.

On a soulless day, as the light gives up the fight, dark descends, the wind rises and snow flakes threaten once more, Lowther is hauntingly beautiful and you can feel the history of the place. The graveyard at St Michael's Church is straight out of Hammer horrors with its mausoleum and frightening carved heads and winged hounds at its corners, the statue of 'William, Earl of Lonsdale 1883' on the top tier and the forbidding doors of the crypt below. I am sure it is entirely different in the sunshine of a summer's day, but on a winter's evening with the graves covered in snow, the wind in the trees and everything grey, white and black, it is imposing. The spectacular outer shell of the old castle adds significantly to an atmosphere of foreboding. I shall be gone!

The church, the magnificent old castle soon have my imagination racing at full tilt over the bones of the old estate. But this was not why I visited Lowther in the first place; it was just that intrigue and curiosity got the better of me. The real reason I was there was to make the acquaintance of Lowther's oldest living inhabitant. This is an oak tree (Quercus robur) which is also known as Jack's Yak (oak) or, alternatively, the Towd (old) Yak. The tree is impressive and, again, it's a little eerie and there are shades of Sleepy Hollow, of the headless horseman variety, when the mist is on the land. The tree is situated on a corner just down the way from the Lowther estate offices. It is unmistakeable, not least because of the four main limbs that emanate from its gnarled and ancient trunk. One is not unlike a switchback and is supported at the lowest point of its U shape by three wooden props a couple of feet above the ground. Superstition has it that if a branch hits the ground the fortunes of the Lowther family – which has lived here since 1283 when King Edward 1 granted the right to 'impark' an area of Lowther – will take a dip or, in the worst-case scenario, the Earl of Lonsdale will fall. This is, of course, poppycock.

Jack's Yak is 400 to 500 years old but who Jack was and how the tree got its name is something of a mystery. The oak is one of a number of veterans on the 3,500-

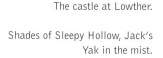

The castle at Lowther.

Shades of Sleepy Hollow, Jack's Yak in the mist.

acre Lowther home estate, parkland that is blessed with many fine trees. Here, for example, on a footpath linking Lowther to Eamont Bridge along the River Lowther, are statuesque beech said to have been grown from seedlings taken from the Foret de Soigne after the Battle of Waterloo in 1815. The story has it that a member of the Lowther family was a lieutenant in Wellington's army and, in the days following the battle, he and fellow officers entered the nearby Foret de Soigne where he was so impressed by the beech trees that he collected seedlings and brought them home to the estate where they were planted by the river.

Other Lowther trees are also well travelled. The pines on the opposite side of the river to the showfield arena were initially grown in Barbados where, in the 18th Century, the then Earl of Lonsdale was a plantation owner and sometime governor of the island. He planted seedlings from Scots pine taken from Lowther in and around his residence in the West Indies and, on his return to England, brought the young pines back with him and replanted them at Lowther.

It is not known which climate the pines preferred. But on a cold winter's evening at Lowther I have no doubt at all where I would rather be.

## An oak near Dufton

If only trees had eyes. An old oak that stands sentinel deep in the Eden Valley is ideally placed to watch the world go by. It stands on a high point set back from the narrow road leading from Appleby to Dufton. The tree is remarkable because of the spread and reach of its roots, each an anaconda on the move down a slope of rich-red soil. The tree, although not big as oaks go, appears taller because of its position at the top of the hillock on which it stands.

On one side is the expanse of the Eden Valley with fields interspersed by scattered villages and farmsteads, hedges, walls, woodland, streams and ditches that reach out as far as the saddleback summit of Blencathra in the distance. On the other is the backbone of England, the Pennines, home of the Helm Wind that when it blows in winter can freeze the ears off a hare.

I chose to visit the oak late one autumnal evening, in that often-magical time slot when the light fades and nature pauses for a while before darkness covers the land and your eyes adjust to vision via moonlight. The silence is wrecked by the raucous cry of pheasants as they suddenly break cover, all wings and blaring cacophony, struggling to be airborne, low flying bombers about to crash land in the next field.

Rabbits decorate a nearby hillside, bunny hopping about or making a dash for the burrow if alarmed and cautiously reappearing when all is clear. Just beyond the oak is a field of maize and through the stems of the seemingly wasted crop I see the red surround of a pheasant's eye and its head and neck plumage, flashing green and blue in the last of the sunlight.

As the light fades rapidly, smoke rises from the chimney of a house about a mile away and the lights of a tractor slice this way and that in the farmyard on the hill. I lean quietly against the tree trunk for a while longer, hoping that a badger might appear from one of the setts nearby. But the reek of man is probably too strong.

My patience recedes as the damp seeps into collar and cuff and I make my way down the cut beside the oak tree and its triffid-like roots. The car engine starts first time, the headlights of the car light the way ahead and I drive off into the night, building up speed and turning the heater dial to max red.

The oak will most probably still be standing, rooted to the land, many years from now. But then that's the beauty of trees, they stand the test of time and you plant them for the future, an unconditional gift to the world.

## David Imrie and the wild cherry tree

'I like trees very much, and if I had not been a gamekeeper I could easily have been a forester. My grandfather was a head forester so there is probably some rosin in my blood. But the tree that I like best beside the hut is an ancient wild cherry. It is twenty yards away. In springtime it is a mass of lovely blossom. I have often stopped to admire it when the sunlight made its fairness fairer. Some day not far distant it will be smashed by the storm. To provide a successor I have planted another wild cherry nearby. If it gives someone as much pleasure as I have got from its venerable neighbour, I have not planted in vain . . .'

The woodland glade leading to the remains of the wooden hut where David Imrie lived.

189

These are the words of David Imrie who was gamekeeper on Lord Rochdale's Lingholm estate for 50 years. He came to the Keswick area from Aberdeenshire as a young man of 21 in the 1920s and while working for the estate lived in a wooden hut – without running water or electricity – in woodland near Braithwaite. The hut stood in a woodland glade on the north shoulder of Barrow Fell, at the entrance to the Newlands Valley and his nearest neighbours were the people of Little Braithwaite just down the hill from the wood.

Cherry blossom near the hut.

The good life. David Imrie with book, bagpipes and teapot on an open fire.

Of his life in the wooden hut he wrote: 'I have had more pleasant times in the hut than bad ones. I can hear the birds sing in the nearby trees and the sough of the wind on a winter night is a lullaby. As a building it is more in harmony with its surroundings than a stone built structure. And I can pass the evening before the fire with a book. Some time between nine and 10 I will make myself a cup of tea, then another short session of reading and into bed, at peace with all the world.

'This is a free, almost Bohemian life. I have a certain job to do and so long as I do it efficiently I can come and go as I please. I can return from the Bog (Derwent Bog, an extensive area of marshy land at the head of Bassenthwaite Lake), wet to the knees and nobody greets me with a long face and I can put my feet up on the oven door and read in peace on a winter night without having to consult anyone but myself. As the shadows of life lengthen, however, that freedom may lose some of its glamour.

'One of the rewards of living alone in a hut in a beautiful district is peace, peace to meditate, peace to contrive things, and peace from the empty shams and insincerities of present human society. But make no mistake. I like people, usually . . . sometimes I have been asked point blank why I live in a hut. My answer is that I like to live in a hut; but that is much too simple an explanation for some people. They think that there must be one definite reason for such eccentric behaviour, some episode in the dim past and I can hardly convince them otherwise. A psychologist might give a reason, but I assure anyone that no reason can be found that made me live in a hut. Chance had a lot to do with it really. It was an advert in two Scottish newspapers (adverts for the gamekeeper's job at Lingholm) that took me here and Fate provided the hut . . . the fact remains that a great many people wish to get back to a freer, more primitive way of living. Civilization palls often. People find that others dominate their lives too much. They have to study this one and that one before they can move. They cease to express themselves and they fritter away their days full of vaguer frustrations.'

A local lad, Geoff Davidson, of Braithwaite, has fond memories of David Imrie.

"As a boy living in Braithwaite and always playing in the woods I knew David very well," he recalls. "I also used to deliver his groceries from the village Co-op to the wooden hut where he lived for many years. I had to put the groceries in a wooden pillar-box a few hundred yards from his hut. The key was always hidden up a tree and as a small boy I used to have to shin up the tree to get the key to open the box. Quite a challenge for a 10 year old and, of course, I had to go through the same procedure to return the key. Another of my memories was listening to him play the bagpipes."

Marjorie Dymock, who was personal secretary to the first Viscount Rochdale and for the Lingholm estate and gardens for over 30 years from 1963, told me: "He was a man of many parts – a talented artist, linguist, writer and regular contributor to *The Shooting Times*, a bagpipe player and keen naturalist, what he didn't know about the wildlife around him wasn't worth knowing. Although living alone, he was happy and never lonely."

When he retired in the early 1980s David Imrie moved to a tiny cottage in Braithwaite and lived there surrounded by his sketches, paintings and books. Neighbours and friends kept an eye on him but, having become increasingly frail, he became a resident of the Ravensfield Old Folks Home, Keswick, and he died in late October 1985. He was buried in his beloved Newlands Valley, at Newlands Church, on November 2nd.

Of his playing of the bagpipes, he once said: "During all the years that I have lived in the hut I have retained an enthusiasm for the bagpipes. Not every night but several times a week, I throw the drones over my left shoulder and play marches, strathspeys and reels."

If you listen very carefully of a warm summer's evening as the light fades to dark, the fox sets out from his lair and bats flicker across the night sky, you might hear him yet . . . the Scottish piper who lived his life at the heart of a Lakeland wood.

## Worshipful sycamore and the cedar of Lebanon

The name Appleby in Westmorland is derived from the Norse 'place with apple trees.' Two intriguing trees in the surrounding area are situated in nearby Great Ormside and Little Ormside. Great Ormside is four miles from Appleby and there you will find, in the heart of the village, next to the church of St James, a big sycamore that grows out of a series of stone steps set around the trunk of the tree.

It is believed that a market cross once stood on this spot and that when it was broken – possibly by Puritans at the time of the Civil War – only the steps remained and the sycamore was planted in its place by one Cyprian Hilton, who then lived at Ormside Hall, in 1693.

The church is believed to be the second oldest in the Carlisle Diocese. The first church here was probably built in the 11th Century, being dedicated before 1204. Interestingly, a hagioscope, or Leper's Squint, to the left of the church altar, provided a view of the communion to those ostracized from the church building.

Relics of early burials and a Viking sword have been discovered in the churchyard together with the Ormside Cup, or bowl, a piece of Anglo Saxon metal ware dating from the 8th Century that was found close to the grave of a Viking warrior. The cup is of gilded silver and bronze and is richly decorated with vine scrolls, birds and animals.

About a mile up the road from the church of St James, Great Ormside, there is Little Ormside. In the garden of a farmhouse, the Lodge, is a Cedar of Lebanon. General Whitehead, a former resident of the Lodge, carried the sapling in his hat back from the Middle East. Water was rationed on the sea journey to England and he shared his daily pint of water with the cedar before planting it in his garden at Little Ormside where today it stands in all its glory.

The Cedar of Lebanon and The Cross Tree at Little Ormside and Great Ormside, respectively.

## The Holker lime

The seed of a cedar of Lebanon was also sent from a friend in the Middle East to Lord George Augustus Cavendish when he planted a variety of trees in the grounds of Holker Hall between 1783 and 1793. But the single most significant tree at Holker is arguably a lime over 70 feet tall and 25 feet wide. The tree is considered to be some 400 years old and is at its most picturesque when wild garlic is in flower around its base.

Where the first branches spring out near the base of the trunk there is an impenetrable thicket of smaller branches and leaves, a head high jungle that would deter even the most determined of tree climbers. The modern day Lady Cavendish is a fan of the lime.

"It is a magnificent tree," she says. "Wonderfully ancient and very animate. Old trees have tremendous character and different qualities. Some have a lovely atmosphere about them, others cast beautiful shadows and some are curiosities. The lime is very beautiful and is the most wonderful sanctuary for wildlife because it's so dense. It's lovely that it has stood for over 400 years just watching all the changes. It's a venerable tree and by that I mean it's the sort of tree you feel quite humble in front of. But it's also a very welcoming tree in a funny sort of way because it has this tremendous, sinuous-like neck and you can hide there. It's wonderful for children. It's lovely in the summer when it's hot outside because it's cool in its shade and you can shelter in the winter when it's raining. I like to think of the lime when I am away from home."

Lady Cavendish also believes that night time is one of the best times to be among trees.

"If you have a really clear moonlit night there is something so beautiful about it because all the colour is gone and you just get the black and the white and the shadows. Trees look so romantic at night."

## Trees by moonlight at Dockray

A few years ago, setting out at about 10pm, I walked over White Pike, Clough Head and onto Helvellyn in the moonlight with the intention of making my way to Dove Cottage at Grasmere by daybreak. The idea was to follow in the footsteps of the poet Samuel Taylor Coleridge who made this selfsame journey on foot on Sunday, August 31, 1800. He started his walk much earlier in the day and only had to complete the last few miles in darkness. Dorothy Wordsworth wrote in her journal: 'At eleven o'clock Coleridge came, when I was walking in the still clear moonshine in the garden, Wm was gone to bed . . . we sate and chatted till half-past three. W. in his dressing gown. Coleridge read us part of Christabel. Talked much about the mountains . . .'

   To walk at night over the fells you ideally need the moonlight. Once your eyes have adjusted the extent of your vision is amazing, so much more effective than trying to make your way with the help of a torch.

Having never previously walked on the fells in the moonlight I found it a fascinating experience, just you and your moon shadow. It is another world, ghostly, magic, unreal and surreal all at the same time. In the middle of the night the landscape is largely greys, soft whites and muted colours – apart from the bright lights in villages and towns and the occasional car headlight far below – and the moonlight sends clouds chasing across the fell and casts shining reflections on the surface of Ullswater.

Sadly, the moon disappeared behind thick cloud and the planned high-level route to Grasmere was aborted in favour of an alternative down towards Ullswater and back through Dockray to Threlkeld on the old Coach Road. The moonlight returned half way through the night and was particularly attractive when it highlighted gently blowing swathes of sun-scorched pale yellow grass. It was also, as you might expect, very quiet with the wind through the trees producing a soothing, mournful effect. In Dockray there was a unique light show as the big white O of the moon cast the constantly moving reflections of wind-stirred branches onto the white washed walls of cottages.

## The Giant Tree at Thirlmere

The location of The Giant Tree (Silver Fir Abies alba Pectinata) in the forest above Thirlmere is quiet with very little bird song. The place has a sombre feel. The tree, about 100 yards up the forest from the road on the Armboth side of the lake, is situated next to a dry stone wall that is covered with moss and stained yellow with lichen. An old black and white photograph, taken of the tree in 1947, shows the self same wall and the figure standing against the fir gives a good indication of the tree's size.

The main branches of the tree emerge at right angles to the trunk and then, as if they have suddenly hit a wall, shoot directly upwards. It is almost as though the branch has tired of growing sideways or has developed delusions of grandeur and has decided to become a tree in its own right. The branch, in effect, has become a social climber, thrusting its way towards the canopy in pursuit of light.

In contrast to this, other less aspirational branches seem content to dip towards the ground where they are in touching distance of dried and broken twigs and the

blanket of orange leaves, brittle with age. Forestry workers have unceremoniously lopped off one large branch.

Down the years the giant fir, planted in 1820, has towered over massive changes in the valley, not least the flooding of the whole area to transform the lake (or, rather, what were then two separate lakes – Leathes Water and Wythburn Water) into a Victorian reservoir, Thirlmere, to provide water for Manchester and area. More recently, the forest has been thinned on both sides of the water to improve the valley by opening up views across the lake.

A few steps down the way from The Giant Tree there is a beautiful little setting among a circle of seven beech trees. It is known as The Cockpit because rumour has it that this was once a venue for cockfighting. The beech trees create an expansive ring – or 'main' as it is known in cockfighting terminology – and it makes a natural amphitheatre for battle.

The site of the old cockpit is a remarkably peaceful place and I find that I am more fascinated by this than the giant tree that first led me here. Initials have been carved into the bark of the beech trees and the roots of the trees are moss covered and a vibrant green, striking against the earth and the russet leaves that blanket the ground. Here and there among the leaves, twigs and beech kernels that carpet the arena, there is the bright yellow / orange of chanterelle.

Chanterelle.

## Rawnsley's oaks

On the road beneath Catbells and overlooking the lake in the vicinity of Brandelhow four oak trees are situated in a field just below the fence. Closer inspection reveals that a stone plaque is set flat into the field beneath them. The plaque reads: 'Brandelhow. The first property of the National Trust in this district was opened on 16th October, 1902, by HRH Princess Louise. Four oaks were planted here by Princess Louise, Miss Octavia Hill, Sir Robert Hunter, Canon HD Rawnsley.' The latter three mentioned being founder members of The National Trust.

The Brandelhow estate consisted of 108 acres of pasture and woodland at the foot of Catbells and was the Trust's first purchase. In 1910, when King Edward VII died his sister, Princess Louise, wanted to make a gift in memory of the king. Grange Fell in Borrowdale was purchased for the National Trust.

The four National Trust oaks in the foreground, in the field just beyond the road, with Derwentwater, Skiddaw, Latrigg and Blencathra beyond.

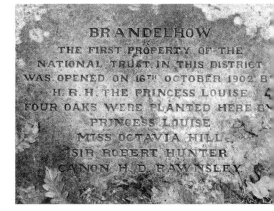

## The heart-shaped wood

A heart-shaped wood can clearly be seen on the fell side opposite the M6 motorway as it runs through Tebay Gorge. The wood has become something of a cause célébre among travellers who would never let the truth stand in the way of a good story. Far be it from me to be an unromantic killjoy but it would appear that many of the stories emanating from this heart-shaped wood and the reasons why it was grown, and in such a distinctive shape, err on the side of fantasy.

The story tellers – depending on which version they themselves have been told in the first instance – would have you believe that the wood is the result of a love story that went tragically wrong. Two families had been engaged in an ancient feud and when a son and daughter of the respective families fell in love – á la Romeo and Juliet – they were denied the opportunity to marry. The young couple entered into a suicide pact (the sensible option would have been to elope together) and met one last time at the site where the wood now stands. He ran her through with his sword before

killing himself. The distraught families were united in grief and planted the wood in memory of the children they had lost.

Alternatively, a second story has it that the wood was planted by a farmer's daughter in memory of her love, a Second World War pilot, who died in combat. It is also said that it was planted to celebrate a wedding and by a farmer to show his affection for his wife. More outrageously it has been said that the woodland's unique shape is in fact not a heart but an artistic impression, a sculpture in woodland if you like, of the pubic hair on a vagina.

Unfortunately, the truth is probably that the wood was planted sometime around 1840 and that its shape is entirely coincidental, that it simply fits neatly into the terrain on which it is planted. The wood was known as the Broken Gill plantation and perhaps the name itself led people to think in terms of broken hearts. Who knows?

I am quite content to go along with whatever a million passing motorists would have us believe. Romance is not dead . . . long live the wood.

# A yew for every child

On the S bend near the 17th century Yew Tree Farm on the Coniston to Ambleside road is a long line of yew trees set against a dry stonewall made of vertical slabs of slate, not unlike gravestones in their appearance. There are 17 yew trees in the line and Jonny Birkett, former farmer at High Yewdale, says of a previous tenant at the farm: "He had a fit wife and he was a fit fella and ivvery time they had a child they planted a tree. Years ago buses used to ga round the corner theer and the driver would tell his passengers the story and you could hear all the old women on the bus having a reet good laugh."

Indications are that there were 15 trees for their children and two trees for the parents.

Yew Tree Farm was owned by Beatrix Potter and was left by her to the National Trust. Jonny Birkett remembers that when he was a child Beatrix Potter would visit his father Robert at the farm.

"Ah thowt she was like a witch," he recalls. "Dark clothes, clasp clogs. We were all telt to sit back and be looked at but not heard."

## ALL SUMMER LONG
### Cricket's mighty oak

*14*

If you were a cricketer who just happened – by some strange quirk of the afterlife – to be reincarnated as a tree what better place to put down your roots than a piece of land destined to be a cricket field? Not only that but a cricket ground where someone with authority, someone who loved the game, would decree that you should remain there for all time or until such time that you fell over.

The oak tree at Lowther CC – a very big six hit from Penrith – has watched a lot of cricket over the years from its vantage point looking out over the Eden Valley. For the first 100 years or so of its life the oak tree, situated well within the field of play at Lowther's scenic ground, will not have had an awful lot of entertainment. Apart from passing wildlife, such as deer, badgers, foxes and red squirrels, or the diversion of a bird nesting in its boughs or a rabbit digging its warren at the base of the tree, there will only have been the relentless passage of spring, summer, autumn and winter, the growth and shedding of acorns and leaves, world without end.

Until, that is, the clock struck 1923 and Captain A.W. Wingate, cricket lover and land agent of the Lowther estates – on which the cricket field stands – decided in his wisdom that it would be a good idea to create the cricket field and the pavilion. Since then, the oak tree (Quercus robur to give the oak its full title) has had cricket to look forward to most Saturday afternoons of the season; unless, that is, Lowther was playing away or the nation was at war.

Now in his early eighties, Lawrence Titterington has been the Secretary of Lowther CC since 1972. He was also the groundsman but gave that a rest in 2001 after 26 years' service before the heavy roller and the mowing machine. A retired clerk for the Lowther estates, Lawrence showed me the minute books for the first year of the club when the secretary was John Peel, a descendant of the Caldbeck huntsman. The club has had only two secretaries in its entire history, the aforementioned John Peel (49 years) and Lawrence.

Not unlike that other famous cricketing tree (the 200 year old lime at the St Lawrence Ground, Canterbury, felled in January storms and replaced by a new lime planted on the boundary edge in 2005) the oak at Lowther plays an important part in games.

Previous pages: A tree for all seasons. The oak in the outfield at Lowther CC with the Pennines in the background. Lowther CC v Arthuret and Esk CC, Eden Valley Cricket League, Division Two, 2010.

The old pavilion at Lowther CC, built in 1923.

If a batsman hits the ball and it comes into contact with the tree then the umpire signals four runs. If the tree strikes the ball then that would be most unusual and we are talking Macbeth and Birnam Wood. Lawrence says that in all the years he has been involved with the club nothing really dramatic has happened involving the tree. I am disappointed to hear this. I thought that at the very least a cricketer might have been knocked unconscious by a falling branch or, in the case of a lightly built, diminutive cricketer, sent flying by a high velocity acorn. Or lightning might have sizzled an opening batsman as he sheltered from the rain after failing to make the relative safety of the pavilion atop the slope during a thunderstorm; giving an entirely new meaning to the significance of The Ashes.

"In some seasons the tree is hardly hit at all, but then all of a sudden it'll get hit twice in one match," says Lawrence. "We did have a streaker run round it once. No names though."

Lowther is, I believe, the only cricket ground in Cumbria with a tree on its playing area. There was a cricket ground in the village of Calderbridge, West Cumbria, that played host to a telegraph pole and as the pole was once a tree I suppose that comes a close second. The tree at Lowther, as can be seen from Val Corbett's photograph (Lowther CC v Arthuret and Esk, Eden Valley League Division 2 fixture, June 7, 2010, Lowther won by five wickets) is in the thick of the action, standing tall and proud at either third man, fine leg, long on or long off, depending on whether the batsman is left or right handed and from which end the ball is being bowled. All of which reminds me for some reason of that classic piece of Test Match cricket commentary from the BBC World Service at The Oval in 1976: 'The batsman's Holding, the bowler's Willey . . .'

Lowther CC. Circa the 1970s. Back row standing (left to right) Keith Graham, Bob Griffiths (umpire and former Lowther CC captain) George Stokes, Colin Maughan, Dick Parker (umpire) Richard Utting, Graham Harrison, Martin Little and David Carrick. Kneeling (left to right): Andrew Hall, Brian Johnston, Barry Turner, Andrew Little, Phil Wharton and Steve Pattinson. Incidentally, the umpire Bob Griffiths was known as 'One Short' because of his tendency to fit every umpire's signal into each game in which he officiated. The 'one short,' clearly, was the signal for a run in which a batsman did not ground his bat correctly. Good old Bob!

The tree also has a grandstand view from its higher branches and when the sun moves across the sky and starts to slip towards the horizon in the west, the shadow cast over the wicket by the oak can ask serious questions of a batsman.

"See where the shadow is now," explains Lawrence, pointing to the square as we look out over the ground on a fine summer's evening. "Later on in the season you are bowling out of shadow to a batsman in the sunshine and that can be a problem for the batsman. You don't have the best visibility in that situation."

The view from the cricket ground out over the Eden Valley to the northern reaches of the backbone of England, the Pennines, is spectacular. The soil on which the cricketers play is the rich red of the Eden Valley. Equally splendid is the cricket pavilion at Lowther CC. It is the original building with its heavy tin sheeting roof and wooden walls and verandah, an adjacent tearoom and outside loo – the latter being three pieces of vertical corrugated iron sheeting placed strategically in a quiet corner. I can recall a similar construction at Threlkeld CC where the toilet was next to the compost heap, the latter masking the smell of the former with its own distinct musk. More substantial lavatorial missions, especially if you were batting at No2 and of an anxious disposition, were out of the question and usually necessitated a discreet visit to some far-flung part of a distant field, hedge or wood. It was one of those subjects that was never really touched upon, you accepted the absence of facilities, took off when it was imperative and managed as best you could. Docking leaves always came in handy, but nettles were most definitely to be avoided.

An old roller and other machinery laze around waiting for work. They are positioned on the surrounds of the old pavilion at Lowther, a building that was simply not designed to accommodate today's wheelie bin style cricket bags complete with built-in personal trainer, wardrobe and a range of perfumery. In the good old days there was a single cricket bag containing all of the team's equipment, pads and bats and boxes and balls and all the player had to do was turn up with his whites and boots. I recall that one player arrived at the Fitz Park ground in Keswick with his boots in a paper bag and the self-same player started the season with a new set of gnashers and didn't stop smiling for a fortnight. Another player, John Stephenson, or 'Scon' to his friends, went one better and turned up with his gear in a fertiliser bag. In the case of Geordie Hutton, of Setmabanning Farm, Threlkeld, his boots were hung on a nail in the barn at the end of the season and collected from that same point at the start of the next; presumably after the family of harvest mice were evicted. Geordie's heyday was probably 1967 when the team in which he played – captained by Stan Hackett – won the Eden Valley Cricket League. The black and white photograph of that team in front of the old pavilion at Threlkeld, situated beneath the ridges of Blencathra, is a classic of its kind and Geordie told me the identity of the lady on the front row.

"That's Annie Page," he said. "Mrs Page did the scorebook aw the time I played for Threlkeld (more than 30 years). Home and away she nivver missed. She was a great supporter of the cricket club. She lived in the village and her husband Harry would play at ya time and her son Bobby. The club was well supported in the Fifties and Sixties and we always had a bus for away matches, a 32-seater, and we always had a bus full of supporters.

"I started playing in 1951 but there wasn't a league then. It was aw friendly games but we had a full fixture list. We went to Ambleside, Hawkshead and we went to Barrow once a year. Then the Eden Valley League started and we went to places like Patterdale, Lowther, Nunwick, Culgaith – nice la'll ground yon – Temple Sowerby,

Threlkeld CC. Eden Valley League champions 1967. Standing (left to right) Bill Robinson, Brian Airey, Stan Airey, Bill Hebson, David Mart, Bill Airey, Stan Airey. Seated (left to right) Wilf Airey, John Bowe, George Hutton, Mrs Annie Page, Stan Hackett, 'Big' Bill Hebson, Les Thompson.

and Gamblesby. The best teas were at Gamblesby where all the Littles played. We went down to the farmhouse near the ground and the old lady theer put on a real spread. I was always keen o' blackcurrant cake. This particular day there were these blackcurrant cakes and I said I had nivver tasted better and she fetched me an extra bit. And then next year when Threlkeld were theer she had med yan specially for me!" Ah those were the days . . .

The pavilion at Lowther may be small in size but it is immense in character and the facilities are completed by a couple of taps and sinks in which it would be indiscreet, downright uncomfortable and impractical to sit and bathe at the end of a game. Around the walls are assorted photographs, some old, some less so, and a wall chart produced sometime around the end of the Second World War by *Empire News* and showing the batting, fielding and bowling techniques as practiced by the one and only Cyril Washbrook, of Lancashire and England.

Nearby hangs an immaculate navy blue blazer with the Lowther CC badge on the breast pocket. The Lowther CC captain wears the blazer when he goes out to the middle with his opposite number to flip a coin before start of play  – in the best traditions of international cricket captains everywhere. It is a lovely touch. In many respects Lowther CC and its ground and the oak tree epitomise what Eden Valley Cricket is all about. It is full of character and if there is a better league in which to play village cricket in such wonderful surroundings then I have still to make its acquaintance.

The grounds, the pavilions and the people are priceless in this commercially crazy world. There is, quite simply, nothing to compare with playing cricket at grounds such as, in no particular order, Culgaith, Gamblesby, Appleby, Nunwick, Edenhall, Temple Sowerby, Stainton, Caldbeck, Patterdale, Shap, Staffield, Threlkeld, Braithwaite, and, of course, Lowther, to name a few. And Morland CC before it, sadly, bit the dust.

Some of these grounds now have new larger pavilions which have replaced the assorted huts with their sad seating, solitary water tap (if you were lucky), basic scoreboard and the dreaded three upright corrugated sheets that constituted the outside loo. Staffield CC's former pavilion and ground at Kirkoswald was wonderful in its own unique way. It was situated in the shade of a sizeable oak on the boundary

Simon Jackson, of Threlkeld CC, at the door of the Shap CC pavilion sometime in the 1980s.

edge. The ground there is also encircled by an electric fence to keep the cattle off the field of play and there were occasions when the groundsman clean forgot to switch off the power before the start of a match. The fielding was electric at times.

The teas were always an important part of village cricket in the Eden Valley and, like Geordie Hutton, I can also vividly recall that those at Gamblesby were legendary. They were taken in a nearby farmhouse and were incredibly good with assorted sandwiches, cakes, and a particular favourite of mine, as it was with Geordie, juicy blackcurrant pies that dripped of heavy summer fruit. All washed down with as many cups of tea as you could manage. A young fast bowler on our Keswick 3rd XI team, Roger Horton, once ate so much during the tea interval at Gamblesby that on resumption of play he was physically incapable of running up to the wicket to bowl and had to be rested at third man until he made a complete recovery. This all, of course, gave new meaning to the cricketing phrase 'pie chucker.' The farmer who helped host the teas – I think it was with his sister, Edith – was also the Gamblesby umpire and I can remember him still, a little old man by the name of John Sowerby, in his cap and white coat beneath which he was smartly dressed in shirt and tie. His trousers, held aloft by braces, came all the way up to his chest. He was also renowned for being patriotic towards Gamblesby with his LBW decisions and the closer you got to chasing down a target the further away, in reality, it actually got.

But it was all part of the character and charm that was, and I like to think still is, cricket in the aptly named Eden Valley League; a league where the club that is Lowther CC has a very special 12th man, a fielder who takes to the field for every match, does not budge an inch – unless the wind is blowing – has yet to take a catch and is so keen that you cannot get him away from the ground for love nor money.

Cricket has always played an important and enjoyable part in my life ever since, as a kid at junior school, I first struck ball with bat in the playground at Brigham Primary School, Keswick. Our stumps were chalked onto the playground wall and you were always mad keen to take your turn to bat; there was none of the raw edge and pre-innings nerves that tended to affect your game in club matches at senior level,

Threlkeld players in the dug out at Morland CC.

at least not until you were too old to care. We also played against the garage doors on Windebrowe Avenue. The gateway from playground to senior cricket at Keswick Cricket Club (awarded Loveliest Cricket Ground in the UK by *Wisden Magazine* in 2001) was the junior nets at KCC in the early 1960s when our mentors were an experienced bowler by the name of Ted Bickerdike and his cohort in junior coaching, Norman Wilde. If it hadn't been for these two fine gentlemen – and KCC of course – I dare say I would never have played cricket beyond my school days. Ted lived on Windebrowe Avenue, just round the corner from us, and gave me my first set of proper white flannels for cricket. He specialised in coaching the young bowlers and I recall that he himself had the most fluid and smooth of bowling actions. There was his easy, almost lyrical approach to the stumps, he ran in on a slight curve to the wickets, and at the point of delivery there was a defined but only marginal leaning away of the body from the crease as the arm came over in a smooth arc to deliver the ball with the utmost precision onto an imaginary sixpence just back of a good length. It was poetry. Over after over, 23 he bowled without break in a 45 over game every Saturday afternoon, a bespectacled Ted wheeled away all the summers long and claimed over 1,000 wickets in local league cricket. So he knew his stuff.

Threlkeld players lose their way in the old pavilion at Nunwick that resembled a former pigeon loft.

The junior nets, wooden poles and brown netting, the latter held aloft by guide ropes attached to metal pegs, were set up on the outfield near the boundary edge. Ted would measure out 22 yards with the chain and fix the wooden stumps in the grass and then – wielding a paintbrush out of a pail – slop a big white circle on the grass in line with middle stump in front of the batsman, on a good length, and encourage you to hit it. If your cricket ball bore white marks you felt proud and Ted was happy. As Ted stood behind the stumps at the bowlers' end, Norman Wilde – pipe clasped firmly in his teeth and peering out from behind clouds of smoke (he ran a small tobacconist shop on Penrith Road) – would teach you the rudiments of batting: forward and backward defence, the square cut off the back foot, the hit to leg and, arguably my personal favourite, although the square cut came a close second, the off drive.

The old pavilion and toilet under the oak tree at Staffield CC.
Pictures: Keith Richardson.

We young lads were all aged about 11 and wore shirts and shorts, plimsolls being our token gesture towards anything remotely sporty. We did have use of a communal

215

junior cricket bag with its batting gloves, these being the old variety with rubber spikes on the knuckles, wafer thin pads and cricket protectors or boxes (to guard the testicles) that possibly first saw service at the Battle of Hastings. Our coaches fared little better. Neither Ted nor Norman had tracksuits, trainers or badges although Ted wore a white shirt and sweater, dark flannels and white cricket boots. Norman, on the other hand, made no concession at all to cricket coaching fashion and preferred the entirely casual approach of his tweed jacket, jumper, collar and tie and the like. In fact he cut something of a Wainwrightesque figure behind the stumps with his pipe and clouds of smoke. As youngsters we went home – after a net session with Norman – reeking of tobacco and inviting interrogation from our parents who wanted to know if we had taken to furtively smoking Woodbines. Neither Ted or Norman had any coaching qualifications to speak of and most definitely did not have to send their details to the Criminal Record Bureau – as you do now – for a certificate that entitles you to coach cricket to children.

The highlight for us lads was the annual cricket match between two junior teams that took to the field, to play, glory be, on the centre of the Fitz Park oval. These games were the climax of our summer's coaching in the nets. Ted and Norman selected the two sides and the teams went under the wonderful names 'Bick's Chicks' and 'Wilde's Whiffs', the latter being a reference to the tobacco Norman sold from his corner shop, although equally it could have been a reference to the fact that his young protégés all smelled of tobacco. A KCC player, name of Ronnie Rose, who was 1st XI captain and wicket keeper at the time, entered the fray at one stage and his team played under the more fragrant title 'Rose's Blooms.'

I do not remember much about the games, except that I never scored many, if

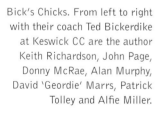

Bick's Chicks. From left to right with their coach Ted Bickerdike at Keswick CC are the author Keith Richardson, John Page, Donny McRae, Alan Murphy, David 'Geordie' Marrs, Patrick Tolley and Alfie Miller.

any, runs, and that Geordie Marrs, another lad off the 'Browe whose parents Dennis and Dolly ran the Avenue grocery store, was virtually unplayable. But they were the highlight of our sporting summer and, for some of us, the springboard for many more seasons of cricket to come. These days there are net nights and coaching sessions for young players virtually every evening of the week and John Bryson Snr, his wife Judith, and a small but perfectly formed team of coaches (winners of the Queen's Golden Jubilee Award for Voluntary Service, 2010) continue the work started all those years ago by Ted and Norman. The club now fields teams in the Cumbria Junior Cricket League at Under 11, Under 13 and Under 15 age levels. There is also a Girls' XI. How times have changed since the days of 'Bick's Chicks', 'Wilde's Whiffs' and 'Rose's Blooms.' And instead of just plimsolls all the youngsters have the right clothing and gear. One of them may even go on to play for England and win the Ashes!

Keswick Cricket Club was founded in the early 1880s when the Hewetson family created Fitz Park for the leisure and sporting use of the town and its people. An old cricket pavilion served the club for many years until the mid 1990s when it was reduced to a state of serious decay and standards of health, safety and hygiene were far from exemplary; highlighted by the fact that a team of visiting cricketers went down with the KCC derivation of Delhi belly after a tea prepared by the home players

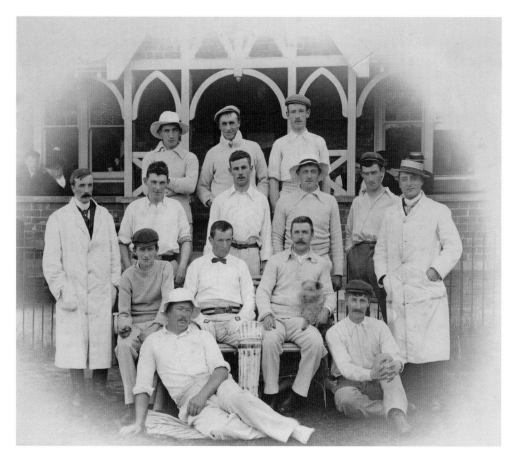

Keswick CC. This photograph was taken by G.P. Abraham. Picture courtesy of Susan Steinberg, granddaughter of Ashley Abraham who, with his brother George, was a pioneer mountaineer / photographer with a business in Keswick.

went sadly wrong. The cause may or may not have been a bottle of salad cream that had been gently festering and biding its time in a tearoom cupboard since the 1880s. The old pavilion was demolished (not, I hasten to add, as a direct result of the salad cream incident) but by a desire to create a new facility more in keeping with the times. Several years of increasingly adventurous fund raising by the cricket club and a grant from Keswick Town Council resulted in a new, much bigger building being opened in 1995. The distinctive curved wooden facing to the front of the former pavilion was retained as a link with the past. This fine piece of Victorian architecture can be seen as a backcloth on team pictures which were taken outside the pavilion and date back to the early 1900s and, in some instances, the late 1800s. Some of these pictures, currently on the wall of the pavilion tearoom (the Ted Bickerdike tearoom as it is now) were taken by the Abraham Brothers, George and Ashley, pioneering mountaineers and photographers both, whose interests clearly extended to cricket (they appear on one of the team pictures); a game that requires subtle skills and that, at its most complex, is the equal of a game of chess between two grandmasters. At its simplest level the game is good fun to play and to watch, especially with beer in hand on a blue-sky afternoon.

Geordie Hutton, captain of Threlkeld CC, much preferred to keep the game simple, and when setting a field for his team he is once rumoured to have told his players: "Same as last week lads but spread out a bit mair."

While buildings and facilities are important – and Keswick CC enjoys magnificent views of the surrounding fells – a cricket club is really made up of characters:

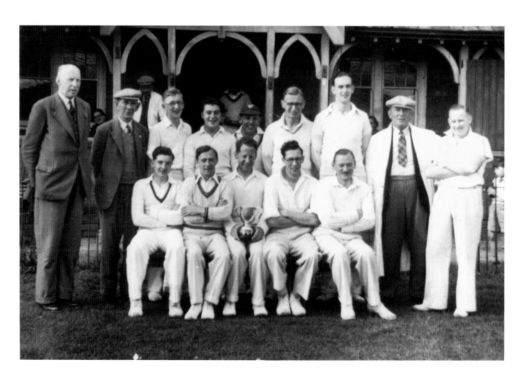

The Keswick 1st XI of 1951 that won the old Cumberland Senior Cricket League title.
Back row
(left to right) standing: Colonel Morton, Sid Stanley (scorer) Ian Forsyth, Bobby Elliott, Derry Saul, Frank Sydney, Wilf Arnold, Harold Downie, and Jack Walker.
Front row
(left to right) seated: Bobby Evans, Ken Sherwin, Alan Jenner (captain with the championship trophy) Ted Bickerdike and Oliver Rigby.

officials, committee, players, supporters and spectators. And wherever there are people there is also, in no particular order, harmony, discord, politics, paranoia, envy, desire, misunderstanding, malevolence, kindness, understanding, madness, sanity, breakdown, co-operation, helpfulness, idleness, energy, mischief, humour, leadership, laughter, tears, loss, joy, vision, ignorance, creativity, sadness, generosity, greed, appreciation, war and peace . . . in fact all of the qualities, or otherwise, that embody what it means to be human and a signatory to the characteristics that are at some point, and very occasionally all at the same time, to be found within any one group of people or an individual.

In my lifetime as a cricketer at Keswick CC and further afield – I also played for a few seasons at Geordie Hutton's club Threlkeld, four miles up the road from Keswick, and one season each at St Bees, Kendal and Cockermouth – one of the characters that I came across was Keswick Cricket Club's former player, groundsman and 1st XI scorer, Brian Pattinson. Sadly Brian is no longer with us, although his ashes are under the patio on what is described as the KCC pavilion's Western Terrace, right beneath the window where he sat for many weekends completing the 1st XI scorebook.

As a young man Brian played for Keswick. He was a fast bowler and as he walked back to his mark would flick his Brylcreemed hair in the style of Fred Trueman. With a whirlwind action he delivered the ball at great velocity and his appeal, when it came, was blood curdling. He once recorded figures of 9/53 against Cleator Cricket Club on Fitz Park. But it was as Keswick's head groundsman (or Head of Grass) and 1st XI scorer that "Patty" became more widely known in local cricketing circles.

In common with other groundsmen the world over, he believed that lovingly prepared cricket pitches were far too good to actually play on. Brian was not always known for his diplomacy and made an art of being cantankerous. He was a severe critic of under performing players and modern day standards, or lack of them. For a while he waged war on the 'dog club' that met in the park in the days before poop scoop made dog walking such a rewardingly tactile and aromatic pastime for dog lovers everywhere. And if anyone ventured without permission onto his pride and joy, the cricket square, then that was tantamount to an invasion threat and usually resulted in a pre-emptive strike. I was actually surprised that he never got round to crushing anyone under the heavy roller, mowing them down with the gang mowers, impaling them on a gripe or biffing them over the head with a shovel. In short he could be a right awkward bastard at the best of times. We nicknamed him Blott after the gardener in Tom Sharpe's *Blott on the Landscape* because of his occasional over reaction to events.

It didn't help my cause, or his for that matter, when I inadvertently threw out his freshly made sandwiches while tidying the groundsman's shed. In truth when I came across the sandwiches in a brown paper bag I thought they had been there for centuries. Brian, a chef and barman for many years at his family-run King's Head hotel at Thirlspot, also created the cricketing tea that would end all cricketing teas. The club had a special county cup match against Millom, of the North Lancashire League, and Brian appointed himself to prepare the feast. He spent a small fortune in his efforts to impress, almost bankrupted the club in the process, and the result became known as 'Blott's Banquet.' To make matters worse the game was rained off and the visiting team never travelled.

Blott was blessed with a photographic memory and was a leading light of the local quiz league. He also had a passion for Sergeant Bilko and good Western movies. He loved Ennio Morricone's *Man with a Harmonica* soundtrack in the opening sequence of Sergio Leone's *Once Upon a Time in the West* but his favourite movie was Clint Eastwood's *The Outlaw Josey Wales*.

Keswick 1st XI, July 1968. Standing (left to right) Tommy Stevens, Brian Pattinson, David Marrs, Wilf Pridmore, Dennis Hayes, Geoff Wild, Ann Blake (nee Hutton). Sitting (left to right) Mike McNichol, Ted Bickerdike, Brian Broadbent (captain), Terry Smith and Alan Blake.

During his schooldays Brian and his pal Colin 'Blood' Melvin (Colin's dad was a butcher) took immense delight in taking the piss out of the more extravagant lyrics of local hunting songs. Blood, himself a very good cricketer who wore his battered old green and red Keswick School cricket cap well into his senior playing years, went on to become an equally accomplished cricket umpire and president of the Eden Valley Cricket League. Sadly, he has now joined his old pal in the cricketing hereafter.

After he tired of insulting customers at the pub, Brian spent countless hours at the cricket club working on the ground and was at his happiest when the sun shone and he was there of an afternoon, working on the square, wheeling backwards and forwards along a wicket on the old heavy roller, preparing a strip for batsmen, his faithful companion, the spaniel Skip, nearby. After that he'd retire to the pub to consume a vast amount of beer and enjoy the crack.

Goodness, we miss him now, for all his faults. But then who in this world can, or would ever want to, lay claim to perfection?

Players in the teams of Brian's playing days, the 1970s, liked a few beers on the way to a match as well as afterwards and some – if the opportunity presented itself – would indulge during the game. Legendary among these was one Michael McNichol, also known as McDuff, a wicket keeper who specialised in nudging the bails off with his knees and claiming with an amazing success rate that the batsman had been bowled. In that same team was John 'Shooey' Birkett who ran a shoe shop in town and usually fielded at second slip or gully. One Saturday afternoon Shooey was standing in the slips during a lull in play – I think the fielding side was awaiting the arrival of the next batsman from the pavilion – when he suddenly and inexplicably leapt high and wide to his right, arms outstretched and landed with a thump face down on the grass. His team mates were nonplussed by this unexpected leap into the unknown and as Shooey picked himself up and brushed himself down, McDuff the wicket keeper asked: "What the hell was that all about?"

"I just felt like a dive," replied Shooey, as if it was a perfectly normal thing to do when you found yourself with time on your hands.

Shooey's big mate was Bobby Elliott, top order batsman for many seasons with JP (John Price) and the pair were renowned for various party pieces that were guaranteed to empty the public bar, the one with the wine red walls, at the Pheasant Inn at Dubwath, a favoured watering hole on the way to and from matches in West Cumbria. Shooey and Bobby starred in a double act that involved an impersonation based on the diminutive Olympic weightlifter Precious McKenzie. Bobby would stand by the bar and attempt to lift an imaginary weight at his feet. After several drawn out failures and much application of 'chalk', bending, straining and gnashing of teeth, Bobby would admit defeat and at that precise moment Shooey – himself, like Precious McKenzie, not the tallest person in the world – would walk across, lift the imaginary bar with one hand and walk away with it tucked under an arm. Just like that. No matter how many times Bobby and Shooey performed this routine every Saturday night throughout the summer it never failed to raise a laugh.  I suppose it was the all-action equivalent of the joke about the old empty barn, told in the inimitable voice of Frazer (John Laurie) in an exchange with Captain Mainwaring (Arthur Lowe) during an episode of the marvellous TV series *Dad's Army*. It went like this:

Frazer: 'Captain Mainwaring. Did I ever tell you the story about the old empty barn.'

Mainwaring: 'Um. No.'

Frazer: 'Would you like to hear the story about the old empty barn?'

Mainwaring: 'Um. Yes. Listen everybody. Frazer's going to tell us the story about the old empty barn.'

Frazer: 'Right. The story of the old empty barn. Well. There was nothing in it.'

Bobby and Shooey would also play the ventriloquist and his dummy with Shooey sitting on Bobby's lap and coming out with such classics as "gottle o'geer." Shooey was also the owner of a rather disreputable toy monk. By pulling a lever on the monk's base, the cassock would be shockingly lifted to reveal a throbbing and very large red member.

Other incidents in the rich folklore of Keswick cricket involved the fielder, a keen smoker, it could well have been McDuff, who invariably carried his matches and a cigarette or two onto the field, and one day succeeded in self-combusting after he dived to take a ball and the friction of body hitting turf ignited the matches in his pocket. Various other players somehow always managed to enmesh themselves in fencing while pursuing a ball to the boundary and failing to stop or, in one notoriously painful incident, tumbling into a brick-based bed of nettles at Culgaith. A KCC player, strikingly ashen and gaunt in appearance, once gave a nasty shock to a passer-by who was taking a short cut through the graveyard adjacent to the cricket ground at Appleby. Our man in whites, attempting to find a ball which had been hit out of the ground, suddenly reared up from behind a gravestone and clearly did a more than passable impersonation of a spectre.

In bright afternoon sunshine, so he really had no excuse, former 1st XI captain Brian Broadbent became entangled in a child's bicycle at the boundary edge at Keswick and was abandoned by his colleagues because the innings had ended and it was time to take tea. As the players wandered happily into the pavilion they looked back and laughed at their hapless captain as he attempted to extricate himself from the spokes of the bike. It is, of course, a time-honoured tradition among cricketers everywhere to respond with laughter when one of their number is in pain. Serious blows to the balls, leaving the sorry victim a crippled wreck on the grass, incapable of speech or movement but quite clearly in agony, are especially amusing. With a pleasing use of agricultural vernacular, farmer Geordie Hutton sometimes referred to the testes as the 'stone heap' and when a batsman crumpled to the ground after being struck a painful blow an unsympathetic Geordie wandered across, looked down at the sobbing batsman, and said: "Aye, it's nut much fun when thoo gits yan in't' stone heap."

The most recent comic event of note occurred at Edenhall in the summer of 2010 when a long term cricketing friend, the accomplished opening batsman and very occasional KCC spin bowler, John Webster ('Patty' would describe him as 'a stalwart', parodying a much-used phrase in the *Cumberland and Westmorland Herald* newspaper) suffered the indignity of having one of his acutely slow deliveries – occasionally they failed to arrive at all – dispatched out of the ground and clean over the pavilion where it smashed into the side of his very expensive and shiny brand new black Jaguar. John had, or so he thought, parked his latest speed

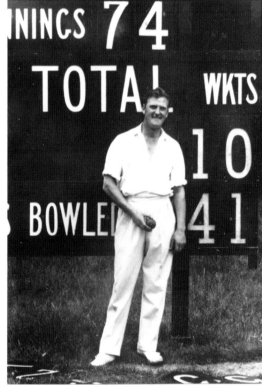

Ronnie Hadley of Keswick CC took 10/41 for the club's 2nd XI in a home game against Carlisle Edenside on July 6th, 1968. Ronnie's son, Kevin, also played for Keswick and was a useful medium pace swing bowler and hard-hitting late order batsman.

Edgar Appleby and Hotspur the otter hound at the boat landings on Derwentwater.

machine out of harm's way. Cricket, however, has a way of finding you out in more ways than one.

Back in the Seventies with the Keswick 1st XI we all, I have to confess, got in some fearful states on a Saturday night because our entire team, plus travelling umpire Ashley 'Tash' Noon, entered into an unspoken agreement that everyone bought a round of pints of beer after the game. And no one left until they had paid their due. Binge drinking, I am afraid, was alive and well in the 1970s. Unfortunately for Bobby Elliott, who lived in Helvellyn Street, he and his wife Ann would take in guests at the time of the town's annual religious convention and would vacate their bedroom to make way for the paying guests. Bobby, returning home one Saturday night slightly the worse for wear, forgot all about it, stripped off and leapt naked into bed with the Conventioners who were almost as surprised as he was.

This raft of assorted cricketing nostalgia from KCC would not be complete without mention of Edgar Appleby - President and Treasurer – who for many years, locals and visitors to the town will doubtless recall, ran (with his wonderful and long-suffering wife Susan) a second hand bookstall on Keswick market. He would depart the stall late afternoon on a Saturday to go to Fitz Park and the match where he would circumnavigate the cricket ground, collection box in hand, and collect donations for the club from the spectators, some of whom were more generous than others; it's surprising how many spectators believe that the farthing is still in circulation. Edgar, a Royal Navy man for 14 years, and who used to open the batting for Hawksdale in the Eden Valley League, would move slowly but steadily around the ground, not a lot of wind in his sails, and as he went would regale spectators with information and anecdotes about cricket. His knowledge of the game was second to none and he also specialised in announcing that the day in question marked some anniversary or other. If there wasn't an appropriate anniversary he would always have to hand a cricketing question, usually relating to the game's greats of yesteryear. For example, why did W.G. Grace declare the innings of his team when he was 98 not out? Answer. 98 was the only score he had not made in first class cricket up to that point. An Appleby grandson was christened William Gilbert.

Edgar's ability for retaining a mass of factual information, dates, scores, statistics and reaming them off, is amazing and he is a very good and occasionally outspoken and risqué public speaker. His speciality subjects, cricket apart, include The Sinking of the Bismarck, The Sinking of the Titanic, the Gretna Green Rail Disaster, the History of the Victoria Cross, the assassination of Franz Ferdinand, The Battle of Midway and, last but not least, the demise of the Habsburg Empire. I often wondered how Edgar went about retaining the colossal amount of information he came out with in his talks, straight off his head and without any reference to notes. The answer, it would appear, was a hound.

I recall that Edgar and family lived in Southey Street and my knock at the door was always greeted by the most awesome baying of Hotspur, the otter hound, a wonderful creature named after the Hotspur of Northumberland. Edgar called the beast Hotspur because he, Edgar, originally came from Middlesbrough, or 'the Vienna of the North' as he called it. Gateshead, where he was born, was referred to as the 'Paris of the North.' Anyway, Edgar would take Hotspur on long walks, or perhaps it was Hotspur who took Edgar, usually along the shores of Derwentwater. I have a photograph of Edgar being towed along a landing stage in a blizzard by a headstrong Hotspur; he had to be on a lead otherwise he would have run amok, Hotspur, that is, not Edgar. As they charged along, Edgar was invariably hauled this way and that but always recited his speeches to the hound as they went, thus dictating them to memory. And so it was that Hotspur the otter hound became the only canine authority on various landmarks in foreign and British history, not least the sinking of the Bismarck.

Small wonder then that this magnificent hound bayed for England.

I was going to end this chapter and this book by writing that they don't make 'em like Edgar Appleby any more. So I will. They don't make 'em like Edgar Appleby any more.

## The Cricketers at Keswick

*On summer Saturdays they weave motifs across Fitz Park*
*between the River Greta and the pavilion boundary*
*where the ground swells to become Skiddaw.*

*Light on the wind and eye,*
*in their mayblossom whiteness they seem like a newsreel*
*of something their grandfathers did in the Thirties,*
*talking at tea of Larwood and Bradman, Verity and Voce,*
*or sitting beneath black drizzling crags waiting for play.*

*Norsemen came here, cleared the land of rocks*
*the last Ice Age had left behind*
*so that cattle could be kept, cricket can be played.*
*They passed the spot where Wordsworth would be born,*
*heard the water's ceaseless music,*
*settled where Coleridge couldn't.*

*Cricketers look up at close of day to see the same relief:*
*Latrigg; Lonscale; Carl Side; Dodd.*
*The sun loops through their lives in a faultless flight*
*Over Derwentwater and Grisedale Pike*
*pitching, somewhere out of sight, onto the Solway.*

*They will wait all afternoon, weeks of weekends*
*for the chance to become their quintessence.*
*The diving catch at deep extra cover,*
*the desperate second run to short fine-leg which wins the match*
*is their vindication, perfection in a perfect world,*
*as nothing else between birth and death can ever be.*

**Bob Horne**
**From 'A Breathless Hush'**
**an MCC anthology of cricket verse.**

## JACK'S YAK
## Many thanks

Val Corbett has made an immense contribution to this book. Having previously worked with Val on two other River Greta Writer publications, *Ivver Sen* and *Joss*, I am blissfully aware of the beauty, style and range of her photography. I think this reaches new heights in *Jack's Yak* and – to use a modern idiom – I was blown away by many of the images. There were so many startling photographs from which to choose that the book designer Gary Burge (of Walker Ellis Associates, Threlkeld) and myself were faced with a surfeit of riches when the book reached the editing / design stage.

Apart from providing the photography for all of the trees that are featured in the principal chapters of the book Val also produced a wider range of tree images. These have found their way into Val's very own photographic chapter in *Jack's Yak*. The results throughout the entire publication are amazing and Val has my eternal gratitude for her work on this book and, indeed, its predecessors. I now look forward to working with her on a fourth River Greta Writer title.

Many other people are to thank for their contributions to *Jack's Yak*. To begin with, thanks to Tommy Orr, of Moor Row, and his party of West Cumbrian ramblers for taking the time and the trouble to visit Wainwright's rowan every 10 years over three decades and enter into correspondence with AW about this tenacious little tree and to provide him with photographs and cartoon drawings of the expeditions.

Reference Shakespeare's Oak at Kendal Green my gratitude to John and Jean Coopey, of Kendal Green, for their time and the research they conducted and included in their excellent publication *Kendal Green – a Georgian Wasteland Transformed*.

My thanks to Barbara Mitchell who first alerted me to the existence of the Rebel Tree at Clifton and to the children of Clifton School for the wonderful illustrations that provided an excellent portrayal of the battle / skirmish of Clifton Moor in 1745. I first came across the school's drawings when they were exhibited in the George and Dragon, Clifton, a short distance from the Rebel Tree. The George and Dragon soon became an unofficial HQ for *Jack's Yak* meetings with Val Corbett and Gary Burge as the book progressed from acorn to print.

Other significant contributions came from those people who were witness to or who took part in events at Clifton Moor during the Jacobite Rebellion. I am thankful they took the trouble to write it all down. Later on, one Henry Penfold, writing in 1904 in the *Transactions* of the Cumberland and Westmorland Antiquarian and Archaelogical Society, provided some invaluable detective work on the Capon Tree at Brampton, a tree linked for all time to events of 1745 and what followed.

Other individuals and organisations I would like to recognise include: Jane King, Frances Lincoln and *Cumbria* magazine in relation to the use of A.W.'s words and correspondence on his rowan; The Wordsworth Trust; Susan Steinberg for the photographs by George and Ashley Abraham (Ashley being Susan's grandfather) of cricketers at Keswick; an extract from Norman Nicholson's poem *Halley's Comet*, courtesy of *Collected Poems* (Faber and Faber); Peter Phillips, artist, for the painting of Sycamore Gap on Hadrian's Wall; Bob Jopling, of St Bees, for his research on the sinking of the *Luigi Olivari*, in 1879, off Braystones; The Beacon at Whitehaven and Charlotte Stead for material on West Cumbria's maritime history; the County Archive offices in Whitehaven, for its research facility; *The Whitehaven News* for the report on the story of Tom Hurd's Rock; photographer Gary Randall, of Brightwood, Oregon, USA for the stunning image of the wreck of the Maryport-built *The Peter Iredale* on the Oregon Coast; David Imrie's biography *Lakeland Gamekeeper* for its insight into his life in a wooden hut in woodland at the entrance to Newlands; Gill Bulch for a floods image of the River Greta, Keswick, taken on the night when all hell let loose and it wasn't safe to be out, let alone next to the raging torrent; The Margaret Duff Collection for an image of House of Correction Hill, and the gaol at Kendal; Patrick Gordon-Duff-Pennington at Muncaster, and Lawrence Titterington and Ian Jack at Lowther, for their time and helpful information;

Ross Brewster for proof reading the book and last, but not least in this list, Bob Horne for his perfectly-pitched poem *The Cricketers at Keswick* which appeared in *A Breathless Hush: An MCC Anthology of Cricket Verse*.

I have done my best to ensure that all the information in this book is accurate and that work has been properly attributed. However, if anything is wrong please accept my apologies. I will endeavour to correct errors or omissions in a future print run or edition of *Jack's Yak*.

And finally, thanks to the Eden Valley Cricket League for being, in my view, the best cricket league in the world and one in which I have thoroughly enjoyed playing since the year dot. The league, its characters, players, supporters and officials, have over the decades provided me with a wealth of experience, entertainment and material – as a cricketer and an observer – much of which is included in the final chapter of this book which also draws deeply on events over the years at my hometown cricket club at Keswick; a great club among many great clubs, big and small, and home to the loveliest cricket ground in the world, Lower Fitz Park.

**Keith Richardson**

## Bibliography:

In addition to the books, documents, articles, illustrations and poetry listed above I also, as part of my research and to gain a greater understanding of the subject, referred to the following publications:

*Bonnie Prince Charlie in Cumberland*, J.A. Wheatley (Thurnam and Sons, Carlisle).

*An Introduction to Clifton in Westmorland*, Anne and Christine Broadbent and Brenda Dyer.

*A Memoir of the Forty-Five*, The Chevalier de Johnstone (Folio Society, London 1958).

*The '45. Bonnie Prince Charlie and the Untold Story of the Jacobite Rising.* Christopher Duffy (Cassell).

*Culloden.* John Premble (Pimlico).

*Ancient Interesting & Unusual Trees of Cumbria.* Amy Bradshaw.

*The Cumbrian Yew Book.* Ken Mills.

*Wordsworth and the famous Lorton yew.* Michael Baron and Derek Denman (Lorton and Derwent Fells Local History Society).

## By the same author

*Companions of a Kind* - short stories

*Ike* - biography of the West Cumbrian rugby league player Ike Southward

*Ivver Sen.* Lake District. The life and times of the men and women who work the land
(all three above books currently out of print)

*Joss.* The life and times of the legendary Lake District fell runner and shepherd
      Joss Naylor

*Jack's Yak.* A unique journey through time with the special trees of the Lake District and
      Cumbria and the remarkable stories they have to tell

To find out more about River Greta Writer and its publications go to:
**www.rivergretawriter.co.uk**

# JACK'S YAK
## Index

*Now all the tree-tops lay asleep,*
*Like green waves on the sea,*
*As still as in the silent deep*
*The ocean-woods may be.*

Percy Bysshe Shelley
*The Recollection (II)*

*Shelley lived for a while in 1811 at Chestnut Cottage, Chestnut Hill, Keswick.*